Alternative Film Posters
A-Z

Copyright © 2021 by Jeremy Arblaster

The right of Jeremy Arblaster to be identified as the Author and artist of the work has been asserted by him in accordance with the Copyright, Designs and Patents Act 1988.

Published in 2021 by ArtCircus Books
An imprint of YouCaxton Publications

ISBN 978-1-913425-81-4

All rights reserved. No part of this publication may be reproduced, stored in a retrieval system or transmitted in any form, or by any means, without the prior written permission of the publisher, nor be otherwise circulated in any form, binding or cover other than that in which it is published and without a similar condition being imposed on the subsequent purchaser.

Designed & Curated by Jeremy Arblaster
Edited by Blaise Radley
Cover Art by Wallace McBride

Alternative Film Posters
A-Z

Follow us
@az_filmposters

ARTCIRCUS
BOOKS

FOREWORD

Whether it's wider access to graphic design software, the intensification of fan culture on social media, or even IKEA's cheap frames, alternative film art has never been more popular. Fans pay homage to their favourite movies by creating unique posters, title cards or logos that highlight what attracts them to a particular film or filmmaker. By honing in on a specific idea or concept from the film, fan-made posters are as much works of art as works of appreciation; if you know, you know.

There are some superb examples of 'alternative movie posters' (AMPs) to be found online, with websites such as AlternativeMoviePosters.com and PosterSpy.com offering a home for film art from talented designers and artists across the world. Increasingly, a trawl of Twitter and Instagram can uncover some lesser spotted gems from budding designers and film fans alike.

The original idea behind this book came about mainly through Twitter, like all good things, with a few threads here and there highlighting some beautiful alternative artwork for recent titles such as Portrait of a Lady on Fire, Parasite and Midsommar.

With that as an inspiration point, the focus was placed squarely on 21st Century Films, avoiding the need to sift through the thousands of Star Wars posters littering the fan art landscape. And whilst the onus was always designs and their designers, it also seemed like a good opportunity to involve some passionate film writers too. None more passionate than editor Blaise Radley, who has either contribute to or edited all of the written entries, and provided consistent support throughout the project. A real hero.

In terms of the posters themselves, I'd like to say it was more complicated than me simply liking them, but it's not. I like all the art in the book. I think they work nicely together and that's about it. There's a similar style and cohesion to them. Sometimes memorable scenes or smaller moments can elicit a strong emotional response, and I think that all of these designs show an intimate knowledge of the film they represent. That's really all it takes.

I hope you enjoy this collection and can forgive a bit of license with regards to the ways in which I have alphabetised the films. The project has been an immense pleasure to work on, and the kindness of the designers and writers in contributing their time and work cannot be understated. This collaboration has been undertaken solely online and through social media. A very modern project. I urge you to show your support by following, liking and generally supporting the artists and writers featured in the book by using the social and web pages at the back.

By Jeremy Arblaster

WRITING

Contributing Editor-

Blaise Radley - Arrival, Bait, Eternal Sunshine of the Spotless Mind, A Ghost Story, Moonlight, Shame, Uncut Gems, You Were Never Really Here

Contributors-

Jeremy Arblaster - Call Me By Your Name, Midsommar, Saint Maud
Emily Cashen - The Lighthouse, Lost In Translation
Sara Clements - Atonement, The Favourite
Meg Christopher - Carol, A Quiet Place
Matthew Floyd - Once Upon A Time In...Hollywood, Nocturnal Animals
Isabelle France - Burning
Trudie Graham - First Man
Nick Griffin - The Handmaiden
Charlotte J - Little Women
Yazz James - Interstellar
Harry Jones - The Irishman, No Country For Old Men
Peyton Robinson - Get Out
Josh Senior - Knives Out
Toni Stanger - Annihilation, Hereditary
Laura Venning - Under The Skin
Brianna Zigler - The Master, There Will Be Blood

New York Font
by Artem Nevsky

DESIGN GUIDE

Film	Designer
Annihilation	Various
Arrival	Various
Arrival Book Cover	Lara Flesch
Atonement Title Cards	Various
Atonement	Maryse Mikhail & Jeremy Arblaster
Bait	Alex Finney
BlacKkKlansman	Heemin Chun
BlacKkKlansman Title Cards	Julia Harto
Black Swan	Ken Sjöberg & Ksenia Shliakhtina
Broken Flowers	Sam Coyle
Burning	Henrique Ferreira Fernandes
Call Me By Your Name	Mariana Tineo B.
CMBYN Title Card	Visionsinfilm
Carol	Jeremy Arblaster
Dunkirk	Various
Dunkirk Title Cards	Various
Eternal Sunshine of the Spotless Mind	Jeremy Arblaster
The Favourite	Jeremy Arblaster
First Man	Scott Saslow
Get Out	Dalal
A Ghost Story	Ksenia Shliakhtina
A Ghost Story	Ken Sjöberg & Arden Avett
The Handmaiden	Sam Coyle
The Hateful Eight	Bren Zonneveld
The Hateful Eight Title Cards	Jeremy Arblaster
Hereditary	Jeremy Arblaster
A Hidden Life	Maxime Pourchon & Jeremy Arblaster
I'm Thinking of Ending Things	Aisha Servia & Sean Lazonby
I'm Thinking of Ending Things Title Cards	Jeremy Arblaster
Interstellar	Edward J Moran II
Interstellar Title Cards	Various
The Irishman	Scott Saslow
Jackie	Alejandro Hinojosa
Jojo Rabbit	Gabriella Wintergrace & Ivan Zuniga

Film	Designer
Knives Out	Dalal
The Lighthouse	Various
Lighthouse Character Posters	Gabriella Wintergrace
Little Women	Scott Saslow & Sean Lazonby
Little Women Book Cover	Beth Morris
Lost in Translation	Daniel Deme
Mank	Jeremy Arblaster
The Master	Sam Coyle & Jeremy Arblaster
The Master Title Cards	Yudhistira Reihan
Midsommar Flyer	Gabriel Murgueytio
Midsommar Title Card	Gabriella Wintergrace
Midsommar	Wallace McBride & Luke Headland
Moonlight	Ahmad Sindi
Moonlight	Louie Barahom
Moonlight Title Cards	Various
No Country for Old Men	Mathieu David
Nocturnal Animals	Rafal Rola
Once Upon a Time in... Hollywood	Rafael Orrico Diez
Parasite	Reggie Azwar
Portrait of a Lady on Fire	Jeremy Arblaster
A Quiet Place Book Cover	Matt Stevens
Roma	Heemin Chun
Roma Title Cards	Jeremy Arblaster
Saint Maud	Various
Shame	Jeremy Arblaster
There Will Be Blood	Heemin Chun
Uncut Gems	Rafael Orrico Diez
Under the Skin	Jeremy Arblaster
Us	Dalal & Adam Juresko
Vox Lux	Henrique Ferreira Fernandes
The Witch	Adam Juresko
You Were Never Really Here	Jay Bennett
Ex_Machina	Tom Sheffield
Zero Dark Thirty	Rafael Orrico Diez & Scott Saslow

Annihilation (2018)

Alternative Poster by Adam Juresko
Words by Toni Stanger

While Alex Garland's *Annihilation* isn't a Lovecraft adaptation, it certainly feels like one, following five women on a scientific expedition into The Shimmer; an anomalous zone where the laws of nature don't apply. An alien presence changes everything it touches, but rather than horrific decay, The Shimmer showcases hauntingly beautiful growth where plants and flowers grow into shapes of people, amongst other disturbing phenomena. Garland has a gift for taking something beautiful and making it terrifying, which is the entire basis of The Shimmer.

Each of the women — biologist Lena (Natalie Portman), physicist Josie Radek (Tessa Thompson), geomorphologist Cassie Sheppard (Tuva Novotny), paramedic Anya Thorensen (Gina Rodriquez) & psychologist Dr. Ventress (Jennifer Jason Leigh) — are driven by guilt and self-destruction.

The women's emotional problems provide a reason for volunteering to go on a possible suicide mission in the first place, and their emotional baggage interacts with their surreal and unsettling environment. Much like Denis Villeneuve's *Arrival*, *Annihilation* is a thoughtful and introspective sci-fi with lots of hidden layers. It asks some deep questions, ones it doesn't necessarily give answers to. The fear of the unknown will always be paralysing, even when the striking cinematography by Garland's frequent collaborator Rob Hardy and Andrew Whitehurst's visual effects are intoxicatingly perfect.

dir. Alex Garland
with Natalie Portman

"Garland has a gift for taking something beautiful and making it terrifying."

Alternative Poster by Santana López

Alternative Poster by Matt Needle

A R R I V A L

Alternative Poster by Agustin R. Michel
Words by Blaise Radley

Is there anything in human history that's led to more horrific loss, to more senseless barbarism, to colonialism and to genocide, than a fear of the other? By separating "us" from "them", we make cultural and interpersonal differences—the very things we should celebrate—a source of suspicion. Rather than try to understand one another, we ostracise, avoiding the one tool that supposedly makes humanity civilised: communication.

In Denis Villeneuve's *Arrival*, language is everything. Aliens have invaded! Or, rather they're trespassing, hovering at seemingly random intervals across the globe in strange oval ships. The passivity of these squidlike "heptapods" is just as alien to us as their method of communication; circuitous symbols ejected from their tendrils. Unsurprisingly, there are those who infer violence beneath their every turn of phrase (or ink blot).

Arrival moves at a methodical pace, Villeneuve handling each of his knotted subject matters—language as perception; the courage gradual action requires; time as a flat circle—with an even-handed clarity. The fact that its central conflict arises from a debate over the etymological distinctions between "tool" and "weapon" says everything. For once, diplomacy wins out against nukes and lasers.

dir. Denis Villeneuve
with Amy Adams, Jeremy Renner

> "Arrival moves at a methodical pace with an even-handed clarity."

   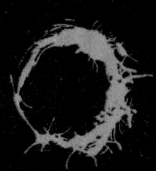

ARRIVAL

Alternative Poster by Ksenia Shliakhtina

Alternative Poster by Cassie Friel

ARRIVAL TED CHIANG

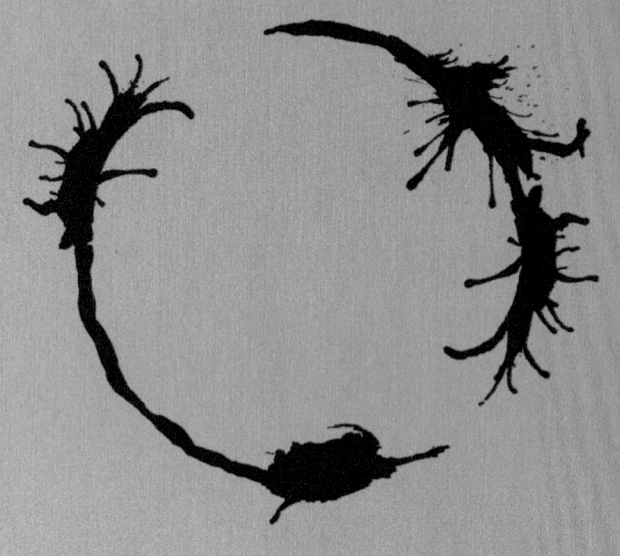

ARRIVAL

Alternative Book Cover by Lara Flesch

Arrival was adapted by Denis Villeneuve from Ted Chiang's short story *Story of Your Life*, part of his collection *Story of Your Life and Other Stories*.

Atonement (2007)

Words by Sara Clements

Alternative Title Cards
Top: Yudhistira Reihan
Middle: Jiho
Bottom: Alexis Payán

Based on Ian McEwan's novel of the same name, Joe Wright's *Atonement* is a masterful work about how a lie can brutally change the course of lives in an instant. Set in a beautiful manor in the English countryside shortly before WWII, the film examines the life of the Tallis family, specifically the relationship the eldest daughter, Cecilia (Keira Knightley), forms with the cook's son, Robbie (James McAvoy).

The film is erotic, packed with intense chemistry between its two leads, but *Atonement* is more than just a period drama romance. It's about how, through the eyes of a child, events can become brutally distorted. This lie and the consequences it presents make for a painful watch.

Behind this lie is Cecilia's sister Briony—the role that catapulted Saoirse Ronan to fame. It's a now infamous character and one frequently cited by those who don't want children as a reason why. Briony is jealous, resentful and naive.

When the film flashes forward five years later, Robbie is now fighting in the war, and though Cecilia and himself remain very much in love, the effects of Briony's actions are still felt as she attempts to atone for the damage she's done. It's a film about lost love, regret, and the power of words. *Atonement* casts a spell that's both haunting and seductive.

dir. Joe Wright
with Keira Knightley, James McAvoy

"Erotic and packed with chemistry... a film about lost love."

Alternative Poster by Maryse Mikhail

Alternative Poster by Jeremy Arblaster

Bait (2019)

Alternative Poster by Alex Finney
Words by Blaise Radley

If every image has a corresponding negative, then the inverse of *Bait* would be an ultra-glossy holiday ad. You know the sort; oversaturated sunrises; cocktails with your feet up; impossibly proportioned men and women to share longing stares with. These ads imply that a land of unrepressed desires lies just beyond the veil, even if that great unknown is only the South coast of England. For Mark Jenkin, the director, these adverts aren't just selling holidays—they're selling out the locals.

The depiction of Cornwall found in *Bait* couldn't be any further from an idyllic postcard getaway. Jenkin transforms gentrification into a black-and-white nightmare, mirroring the displacement caused by holiday home tourism through his caustic aesthetics.

The dialogue is overdubbed, the chronology distorts through fissures in the 16mm film, and contextual reference points are avoided in favour of close-ups. Never has a small Cornish fishing town felt so oppressive.

What distinguishes *Bait* is its harsh sense of humour. The clash between the hoity-toity poshos and the gruff industrious locals is charged with bitter barbs and loaded silences, provoking an even share of grins and grimaces. *Bait* might look like a film shot in the '60s, but the darkest joke of all is that this kitsch invasion is happening right now, across pleasant coastal paths the country over. With *Bait*, Jenkin draws a line in the sand.

dir. Mark Jenkin
with Edward Rowe

"Never has a small Cornish fishing town felt so oppressive."

BLACKkK
KLANSmn
LANSA

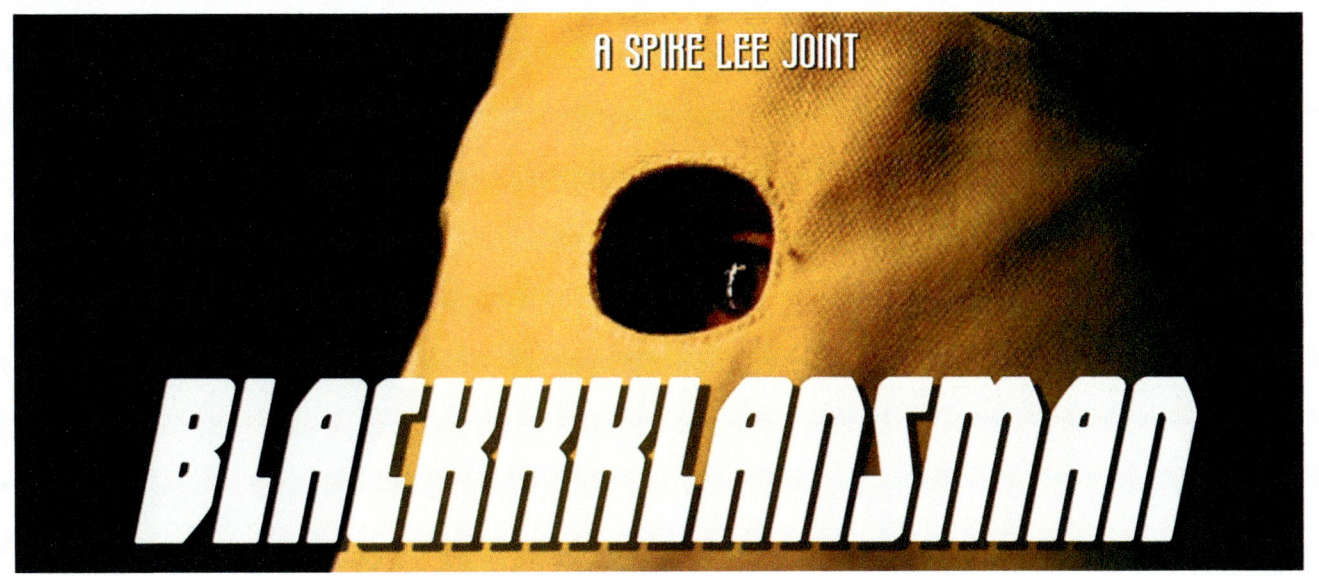

BLACKkKLANSMAN

dir. Spike Lee
with John David Washington, Adam Driver, Laura Harrier

Alternative Poster by Heemin Chun
Alternative Title Cards by Julia Harto

Black Swan (2011)

dir. Darren Aronofsky
with Natalie Portman

Alternative Posters by Ken Sjöberg & Ksenia Shliakhtina

Broken Flowers (2005)

Alternative Poster by Sam Coyle
Words by Blaise Radley

By the time we meet him, Don Johnston (Bill Murray)—or Don Juan as his wannabe-sleuth buddy Winston (Jeffrey Wright) knowingly calls him—has had all his edges sanded off. He's successful, comfortable, and yet totally washed out. We hear about his exploits as a young womaniser, hear about his wildly successful computer company, even see the women who've fallen under his spell, but he appears, to us, like a scarcely-there imprint. Perhaps that's what makes him so impossible to ignore.

What saves *Broken Flowers* from being an exercise in crusty white male masturbation is that it recognises the sadness inherent to such a hollow string of love affairs, but never wallows in it. Johnston is Murray at his Murray-iest, coming right off the back of a slew of poe-faced indie sleeper hits, but director/writer Jim Jarmusch is pointedly aware of that. As much a commentary on the archetypally droll Murray windbag as a contemplation of the changing tides of time, *Broken Flowers* is much too witty to be lumped in with other early '00s hipster snooze-fests.

The trigger for Johnston's emotional query is a simple one—a cryptic note referencing old trysts, and a previously unknown son. As our deflated lothario travels the country to charm and interrogate flings from his halcyon days, his comedic deflections slowly carry less weight, and his stony stares begin to sing differently. What we see eroded is his overriding conviction that emotions are somehow weakness. What we feel is his need for answers swell. The fact they're in short supply makes this bittersweet road-trip sit softly on the tongue.

dir. Jim Jarmusch
with Bill Murray

"Broken Flowers is too witty to be lumped in with other hipster snooze-fests."

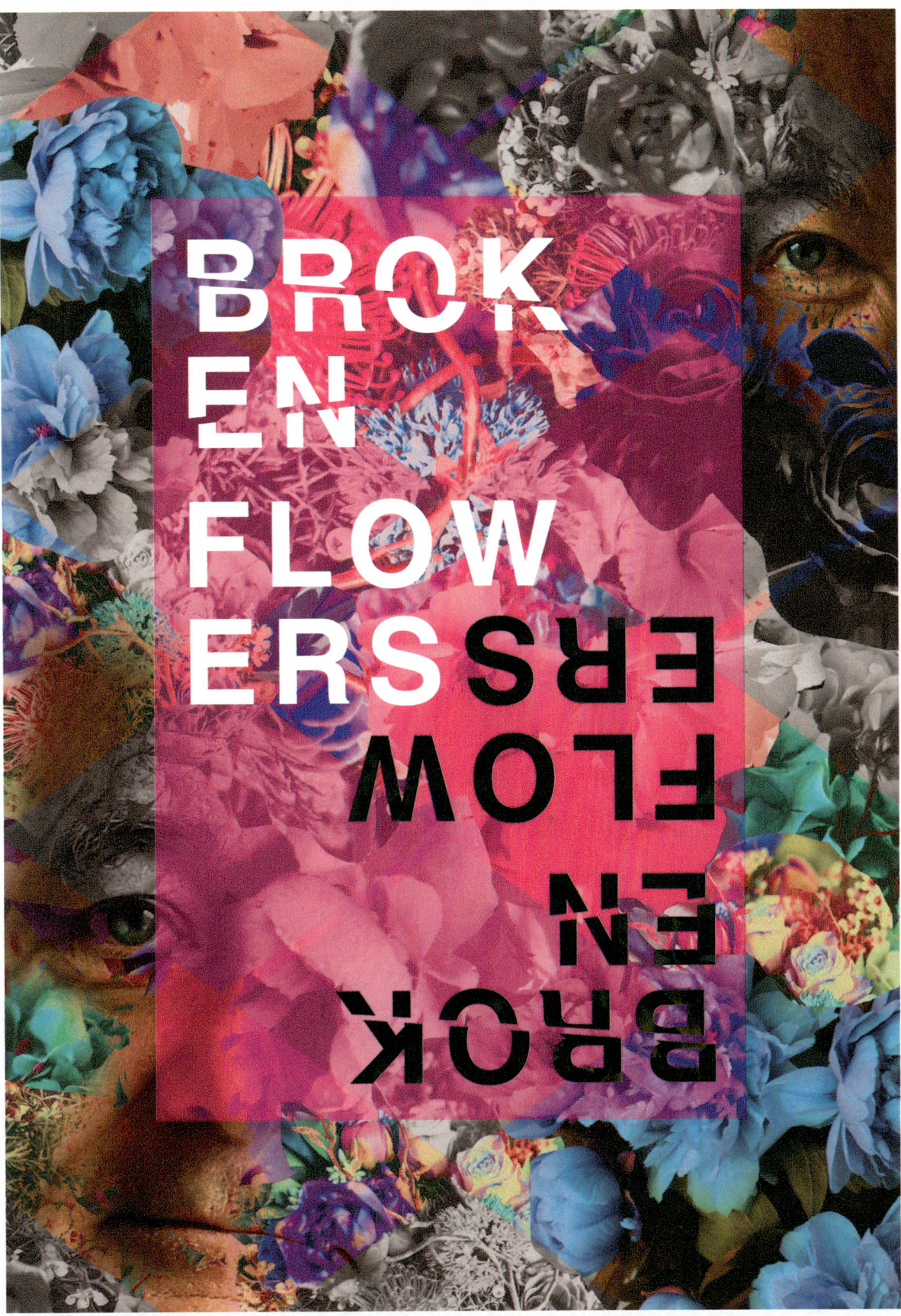

Burning (2018)

Alternative Poster by Henrique Ferreira Fernandes
Words by Isabelle France

Adapted from Murakami's short story *Barn Burning*, *Burning*'s plot could be summed up quickly: boy meets girl, girl meets another boy, girl disappears. You'd be forgiven for thinking this is a romance mystery. But *Burning* is a film full of metaphors, with director Lee Chang-dong providing a sweeping stage for the tussle of masculinity to play out on a beautifully epic scale.

When Jong-su (Yoo Ah-in) reconnects with a childhood acquaintance, Hae-mi (Jeon Jong-seo) in a busy street in Gangnam, he is flustered by her. She is a tsunami of a woman, loud, vibrant—at times obnoxious. Unrecognisable from her youth—although she admits that's down to her surgery—the two quickly strike up a romance; both clearly alone and desperate for a semblance of stability. A rare opportunity in the hyper-capitalist society of Korea. Jong-su is smitten.

He waits eagerly for Haemi to return from a trip to Africa, feeding her cat while she's away, living out fantasies of the two of them in his head, and picking her up at the airport upon her return.

However, when he arrives to collect her it becomes clear Hae-mi's affections have quickly faded and now centre upon a mysterious stranger standing at her side: Ben (Steven Yeun). Not a month or so later, Haemi disappears. Never to be heard from again.

Burning is less a tale about love, and more about obsession, about pouring yourself into another person and altering their reflection for your own requirements. Haemi is an object of both desire and validation. Her subjection to plot device feels somewhat purposeful; it reeks of consumerism, disposability, who wants to own her the most? Her disappearance is a mystery that almost doesn't matter as much. What matters is who got the chance to make her disappear. Who was most worthy of deciding her value.

This film itches at you, begging you to scratch at coincidences and clues, it burns away in your thoughts for days, but all the answers are already long turned to ash.

dir. Lee Chang-Dong
with Yoo Ah-in, Steven Yeun, Jeon Jong-seo

Call me by Your Name

A FILM BY LUCA GUADAGNINO

Call Me By Your Name (2017)

dir. Luca Guadagnino
with Armie Hammer, Timothée Chalamet,

Alternative Poster by Mariana Tineo B.
Alternative Title Card by @visionsinfilm
Words by Jeremy Arblaster

Set against the backdrop of a gentle Italian summer in 1983, *Call Me By Your Name* is a picture-perfect photo album of exquisitely told moments that show romance at its most affecting and fleeting. Armie Hammer and Timothée Chalamet are divine as the would-be lovers who dance around each other with a mixture of bravado and one-upmanship, their connection taking shape in a painfully familiar way. And whilst their feelings are evident, it's not only a case of when will they... but when will it end.

There's an impermanence to it all that lends their romance an aching sadness. In a film filled with sumptuous moments, director Luca Guadagnino gives us some iconic ones, including Armie Hammer's dancing and a particularly fruity peach scene. But he saves the best for last with Michael Stuhlbarg's incredibly touching father-son speech — the best since the Major's in Twin Peaks — and a stunning, tear-jerker of an end credits sequence...

some people change your life forever

CAROL

cate blanchett rooney mara

directed by. todd haynes

based on **the price of salt** by patricia highsmith

CAROL

Alternative Poster by Jeremy Arblaster
Words by Meg Christopher

Since its release in 2015, *Carol* has become a lesbian classic—and for good reason. A magnetic slow-burn, Todd Haynes' romantic drama perfectly captures the restraint of forbidden desire. From their first meeting in a department store to their eventual relationship, protagonists Carol and Therese must balance their attraction towards each other with the obstacles that naturally challenge a homosexual relationship in 1950s America.

Lead actresses Cate Blanchett and Rooney Mara portray their contrasting characters with sumptuous elegance; Blanchett's portrayal of a lonely upper class woman hiding an exhausting secret is note-perfect, whilst Mara embodies the curiosity of a young woman exploring her sexuality for the first time.

Accompanied by an opulent score crafted by the legendary Carter Burwell, every second of the film is meticulous, forming an intense account of the visceral emotion that new love brings. Small glances and words left unsaid have more impact than dialogue ever could. With each meaningful utterance of affection, and each touch that holds such heavy significance, it is impossible to look away.

dir. Todd Haynes
With Cate Blanchett, Rooney Mara

"An intense account of the visceral emotion that new love brings."

a film by CHRISTOPHER NOLAN

DUNKIRK
THE EVENT THAT SHAPED OUR WORLD

2017

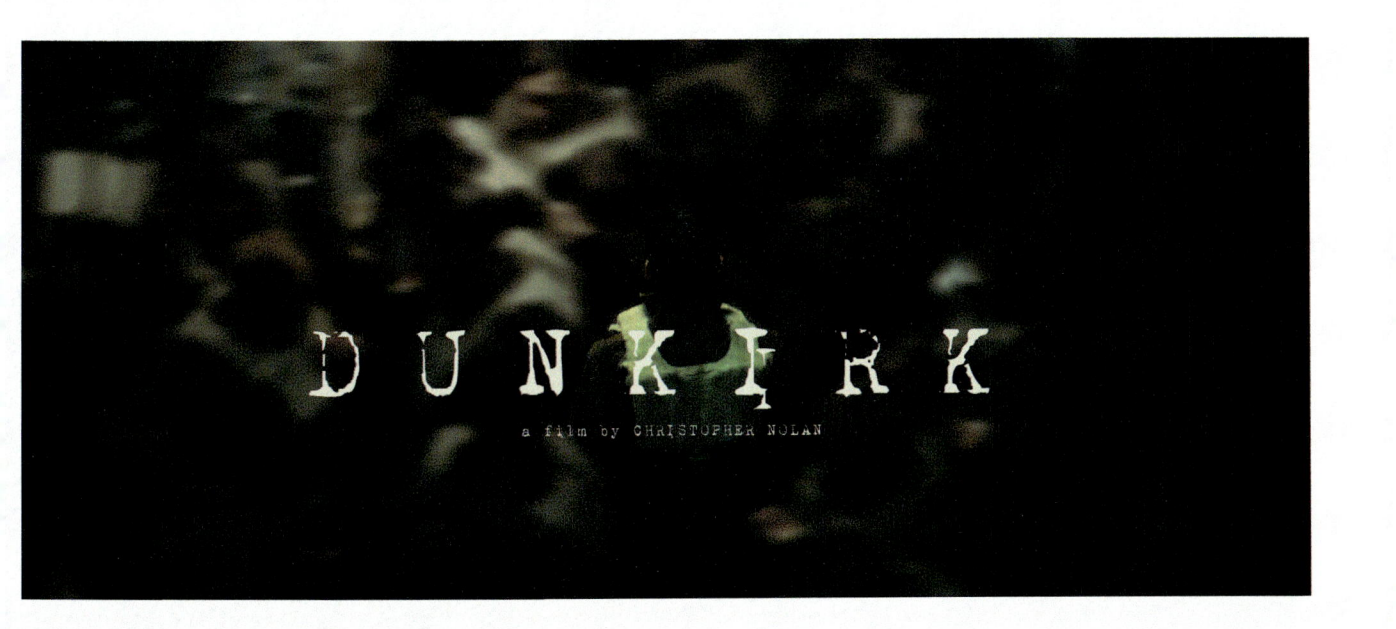

Dunkirk (2017)

dir. Christopher Nolan

Alternative Poster by Gabriella Wintergrace
Alternative Title Cards by Gabriella Wintergrace and Jiho

Following pages:
Alternative Posters by Maryse Mikhail
Alternative Title Card by Angelina

DUNKIRK

DUNKIRK
a film by christopher nolan

Alternative Poster by Matt Needle

Alternative Poster by Anton Volk

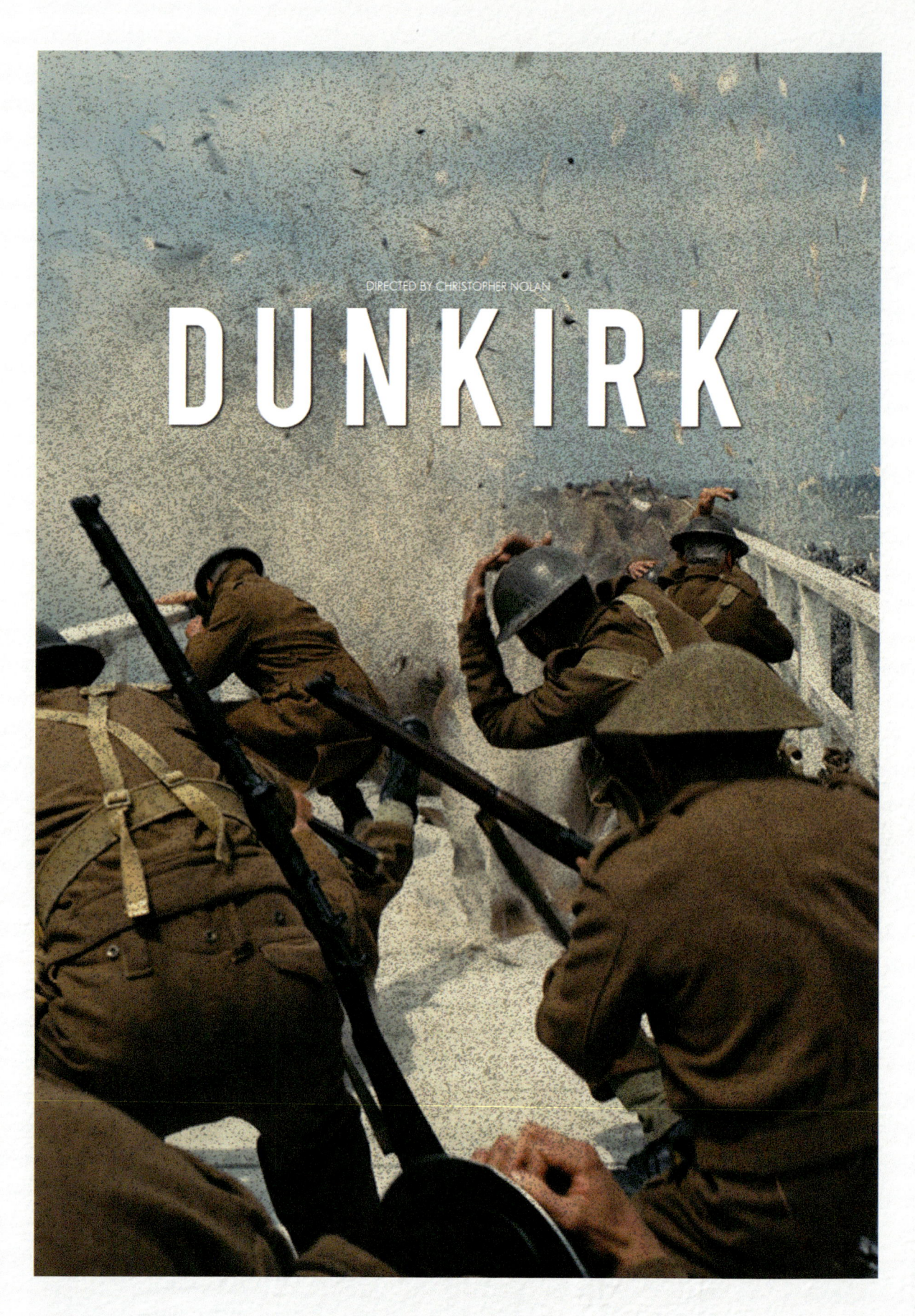

DIRECTED BY CHRISTOPHER NOLAN

DUNKIRK

Alternative Posters by Jeremy Arblaster

DIRECTED BY CHRISTOPHER NOLAN

DUNKIRK

Eternal Sunshine
of the spotless mind

i can't remember
anything without you
that's sweet, but try

a film by | **Michel Gondry**

with | **Jim Carey**
Kate Winslet

Eternal Sunshine of the Spotless Mind (2004)

Alternative Poster by Jeremy Arblaster
Words by Blaise Radley

By its own admission, watching *Eternal Sunshine of the Spotless Mind* is essentially experiencing brain damage. As the film opens, we know nothing about Joel Barish (Jim Carrey), or his equal parts passionate and dysfunctional relationship with Clementine Kruczynski (Kate Winslet), but by the end we've lived through it all, shuffling through the dying embers of their love. For Joel, the very opposite is true—we've just witnessed the surgical erasure of their every shared moment from his mind. "It's on a par with a night of heavy drinking," explains the head doctor at Lacuna, Inc. "Nothing you'll miss."

Filmmaking, supposes screenwriter Charlie Kaufman, is an exercise in memory. The majority of *Eternal Sunshine* takes place in Joel's head as he tumbles between his every shared moment with Clementine, each interaction drawn vividly by director Michel Gondry—or not, as it were.

True to life, these remembrances fuzz and distort, Gondry shifting from static wides to hand-held cameras and stark uneven lighting as the pop-up book world he's created repeatedly folds in on itself. Memories are falsified, actors become disconnected from their characters, and in the end, that warped fabrication is all we're left with: vague impressions of love won and love lost, fated to cycle on forever more. It's one of the most beautiful films this century.

dir. Michel Gondry
With Jim Carey, Kate Winslet

"Watching Eternal Sunshine is essentially experiencing brain damage."

THE FAVOURITE

Leaning more heavily on entertainment than historical accuracy, Yorgos Lanthimos' *The Favourite* is a historical period piece for people who dislike historical period pieces. A film about the power and consequence of obsession, this Oscar-winning period drama is a semi-true story and an *All About Eve*-esque retelling of the hot, delightful mess that was Queen Anne's court.

The film centres on three women, one of whom is Queen Anne herself, and the other two, Sarah and Abigail, who are competitors for her affections. Sarah has been the queen's closest confidant and lover for years, but when Abigail arrives, Sarah loses her tight grip on the court, Anne, and ultimately, herself, as Abigail uses any kind of manipulation to become "the favourite."

What results is an epic tale of bitchery. Deborah Davis and Tony McNamara's script is twisted, intelligent, and hilarious as it explores Anne's eccentricities and the lengths Sarah and Abigail will go through to get what they want. With a cast of powerhouse performances from Rachel Weisz, Emma Stone, and Olivia Colman—who took home the Oscar for Best Actress—wrapped up in delectable Sandy Powell costumes, set pieces, and fisheye cinematography, it isn't difficult to make *The Favourite* a favourite.

dir. Yorgos Lanthimos
with Olivia Colman, Emma Stone, Rachel Weisz

Alternative Poster
by Jeremy Arblaster
Words by Sara Clements

"An epic tale of bitchery...twisted, intelligent and hilarious."

THE
FAVOURITE

OLIVIA EMMA RACHEL
COLMAN STONE WEISZ

DIRECTED
B   Y
YorgosLanthimos

EXPERIENCE THE IMPOSSIBLE JOURNEY TO THE MOON

RYAN GOSLING
CLAIRE FOY

FIRST MAN

First Man (2018)

Alternative Poster by Scott Saslow
Words by Trudie Graham

First Man is a personal drama untempted by the inherent spectacle of space movies. Instead of focusing on the huge scope and on-the-clock tension of the space race, Damien Chazelle crafts a hazy, dreamlike film that completely belongs to its characters, clinging to the Armstrong family's grief and the hope Neil finds in flying to the moon.

The film's moment of clarity comes in a diegetically silent moon walk sequence that's notable in its beauty and cathartic release of pain. To step out into the unknown is terrifying, but this film is about why someone might feel the need to do it, and how letting go of the past is the first step towards allowing ourselves to heal.

Chazelle is content with leaving emotional breadcrumbs for us to find instead of spoon-feeding, so when Neil finds peace in immortalising the memory of his daughter by leaving her bracelet somewhere hundreds of thousands of miles away from Earth, it feels like we're being let in on a secret moment that needs no words to justify its specialness.

First Man is impressive in its admirable VFX, swirling soundscapes, and performances, but the lasting impression is earned by how quiet it is—the bells and whistles of space travel are nice, but it's the emotional arc that makes this an unforgettable journey past the stratosphere.

dir. Damian Chazelle
with Ryan Gosling

"To step out into the unknown is terrifying, but this film is about why someone might feel the need to do it."

GET OUT

Alternative Poster by Dalal
Words by Peyton Robinson

Equal parts side-clenching comedy and psychological gut-punch, Jordan Peele's astounding breakthrough film, *Get Out*, became a shockingly immediate cornerstone of modern horror. It's pure entertainment and deeply subtextual, expertly balancing mirth with mortality. Peele dissects high stakes social issues and analyses permanently relevant themes as they pertain to Blackness. Society's historical habit of the transactional treatment of Black bodies, voices, and culture is pitted against performative, self-aggrandising allyship. There's a constant push-and-pull of power, and a deeply inset air of paranoia that keeps tensions high—even as the events force us to obtain new perspectives and unlearn our expectations.

Get Out thoroughly surveys wilful complicity in oppression and feigned appreciation of Blackness that doesn't extend beyond its value to white life. It utilises "The Sunken Place" as a tangible, poignant representation of society's oppressive fist. It also makes sure to validate that even though the exploitative market for Blackness is ever-booming, the Black vision cannot be stolen or adopted. It is irrevocably owned by the people themselves, and perhaps that power is what's so envied and intimidating. *Get Out* is a film to satisfy both types of horror fans: those who want pure entertainment and those who wish to dive deep into underlying analysis. It's this duality, combined with the film's social stamp on contemporary culture, that makes *Get Out* an irrefutable modern classic only three years after its release.

dir. Jordan Peele
with Daniel Kaluuya

"The Black vision cannot be stolen or adopted... It is owned by the people."

FROM THE MIND OF JORDAN PEELE

GET OUT

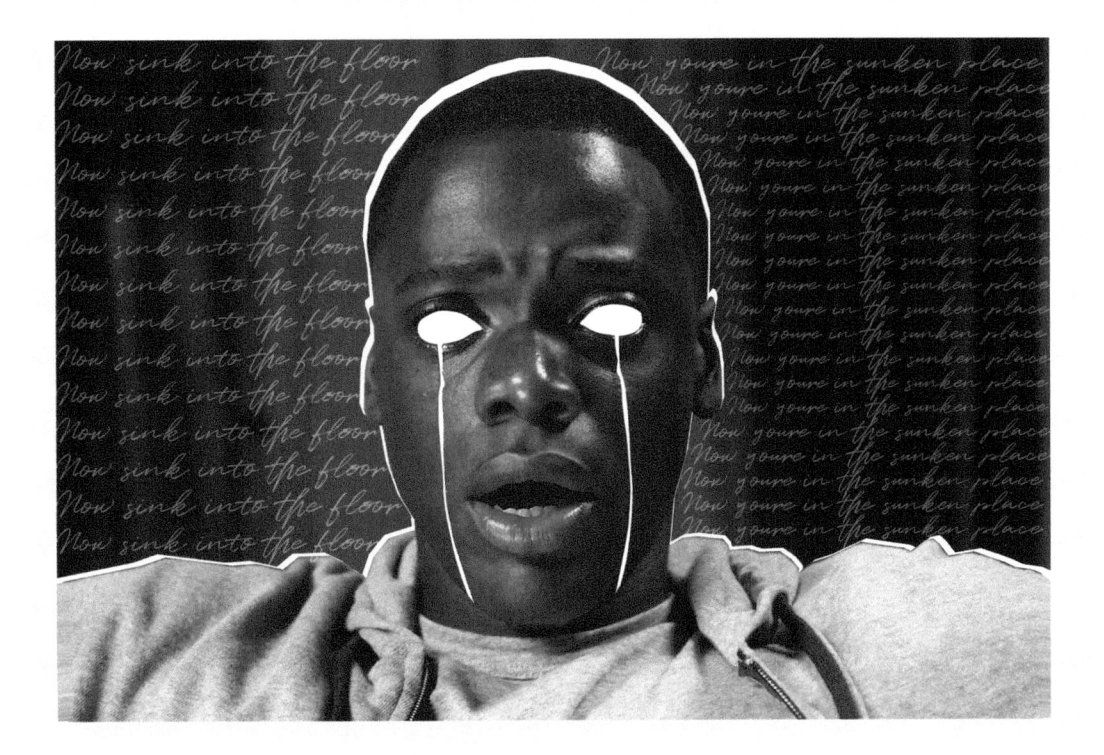

DANIEL KALUUYA - ALLISON WILLIAMS - BRADLEY WHITFORD - CATHERINE KEENER - CALEB LANDRY JONES - & LIL REL HOWRY

WRITTEN BY JORDAN PEELE - DIRECTED BY JORDAN PEELE - A BLUMHOUSE PRODUCTION

A GHOST STORY

Not much happens for the most part in David Lowery's haunted house drama, *A Ghost Story*. Things do go bump in the night, but the haunting is less of the doors-banging, lightning-crackling variety, and more of a mundane, crying-in-your-underwear existential crisis. Yes, there's a ghost, and yes, it's Casey Affleck silently observing his grieving girlfriend under a sheet, but rather than tall tales told around campfires, Lowery instead draws upon the untold stories left by the deceased.

Shot entirely in the boxy 1:33:1 Academy ratio, albeit with vignetted edges, each frame evokes the nostalgia of old photographs, piled high in a forgotten cardboard box. This framing changes the patently silly sheet ghost into something ethereal, making each moment imposed upon by Affleck's Halloween ghoul chilling rather than comedic. By recalling the image of a lost child on Halloween, Affleck's every morbid movement becomes imbued with a deep melancholy.

More than anything else, Lowery recognises that cinema is allowed to be boring. As a medium defined by empathy, an audience doesn't always need to be entertained, so long as they feel *something*. Sometimes it's okay, productive even, to just sit down with a collection of dog-eared photographs.

dir. David Lowery
with Casey Affleck, Rooney Mara

"David Lowery draws upon the untold stories left behind by the deceased."

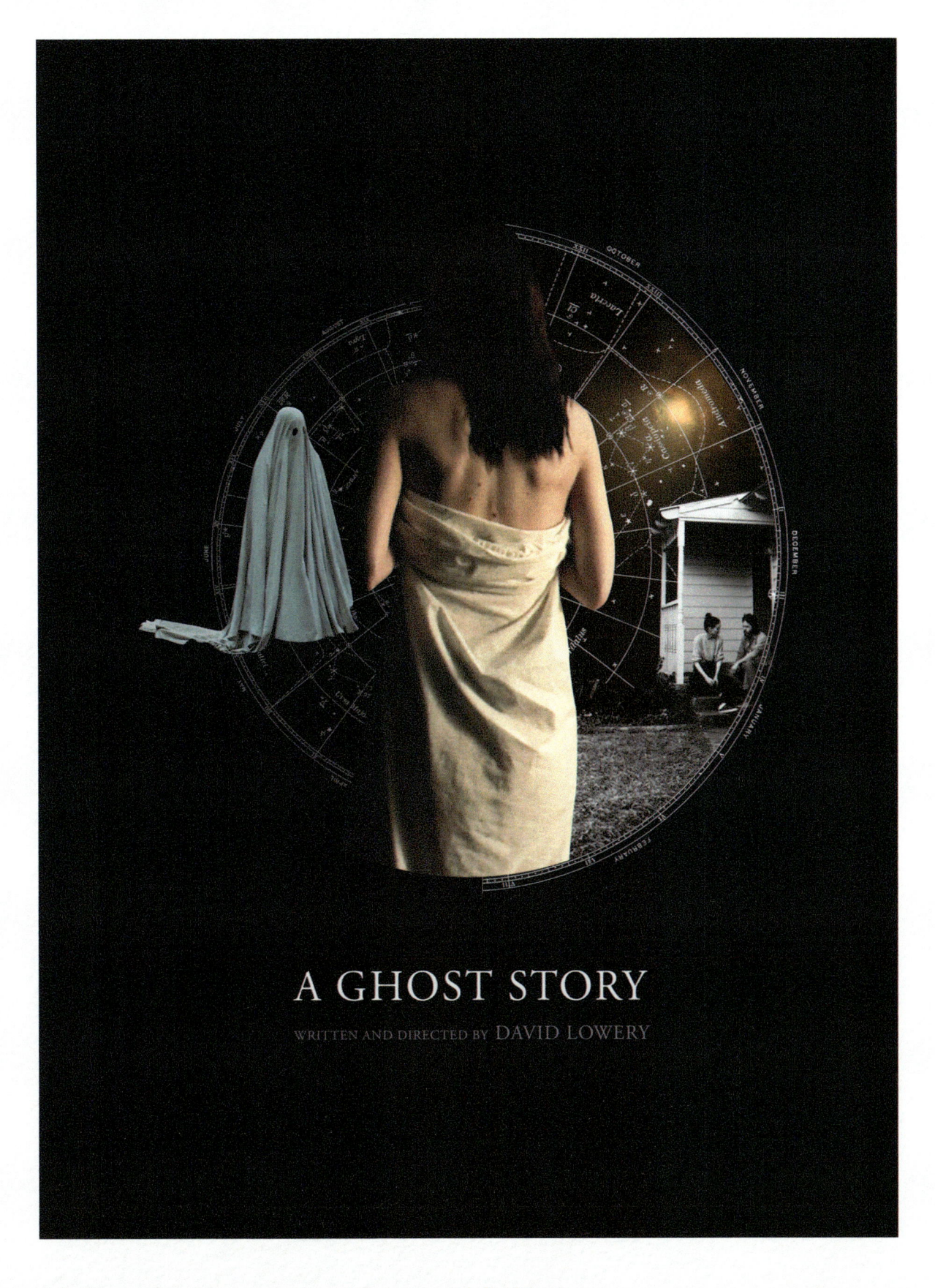

Alternative poster by Ksenia Shliakhtina
Words by Blaise Radley

Alternative Poster by Arden Avett

Alternative Poster by Ken Sjöberg

The Handmaiden (2016)

Alternative Poster by Alejandro Hinojosa
Words by Nick Griffin

Something lurks in the basement in Park Chan-wook's *The Handmaiden*, a gothic descent into the heart of the id. As with his Vengeance Trilogy, Wook is concerned here with dark human themes, tackling the murky, forbidden plain of erotic desire. Spying eyes and hidden impulses create an atmosphere of voyeurism which, as in Hitchcock's *Rear Window*, implicates the film's audience as much as its cast.

This deeply illicit nature is held within a matryoshka doll plot. As layer upon layer is removed, we venture further and further into the prohibited zones of the human psyche. And yet, while these zones are forbidden, and their expression is shown to result in some horrifying acts, they are not presented as something to wholly fear. Instead, what is ultimately suggested is a liberating proposition; these desires can only be addressed through exposure.

Adapted from Sarah Waters' Neo-Victorian novel *Fingersmith*, Wook transposes the action from 19th century London to Japanese-occupied South Korea, provoking conflict between Western Gothic and sensuous Eastern sensibilities. From the level of character to setting, plot to mood, *The Handmaiden* is a film of uneasy and unexpected companionship.

dir. Park Chan-wook
with Kim Min-hee, Kim Tae-ri

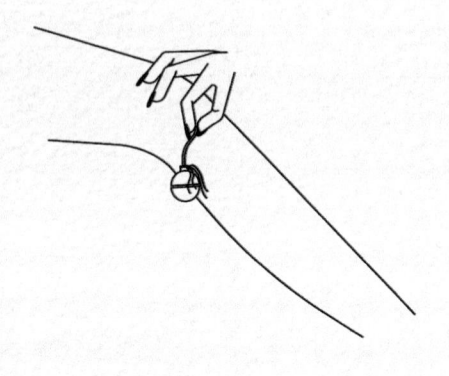

"Wook tackles the murky, forbidden plain of erotic desire."

Illustration by Isabelle France

아가씨

2016 박찬욱 감독 작품

GOT ROOM FOR ONE MORE?
THE HATEFUL EIGHT

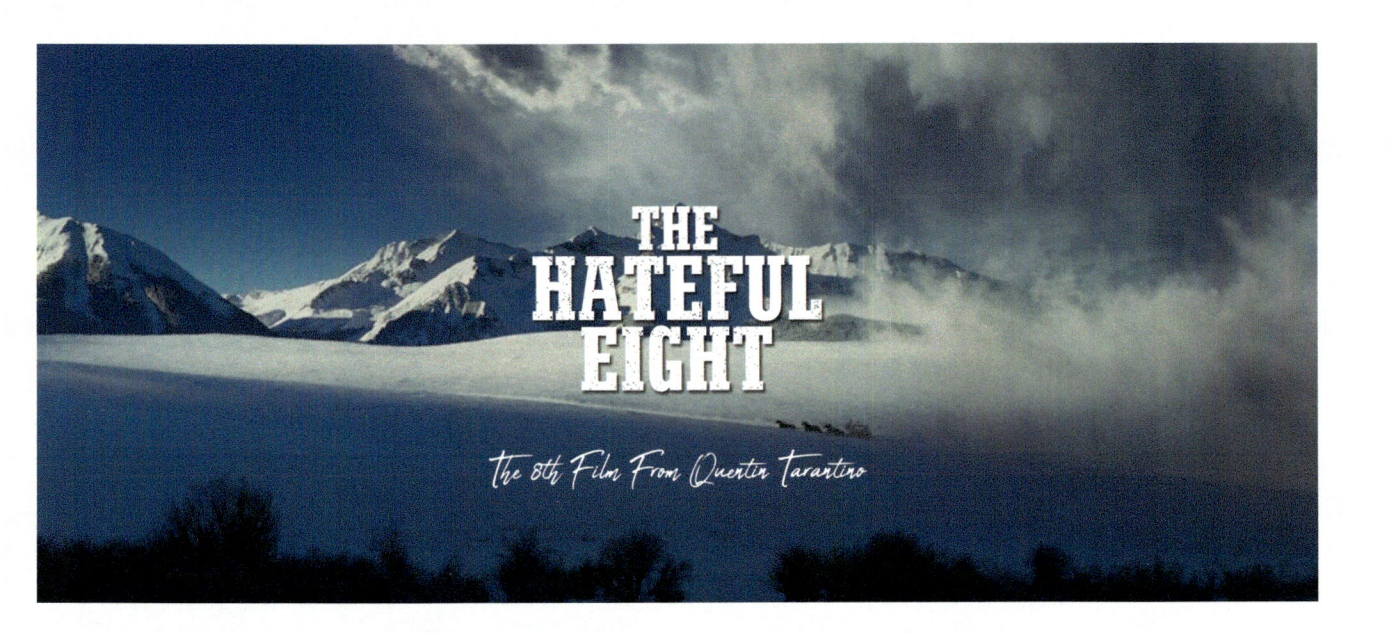

The Hateful Eight (2016)

dir. Quentin Tarantino
with Samuel L. Jackson, Kurt Russell, Jennifer Jason Leigh

Alternative Poster by Bren Zonneveld
Alternative Title Cards by Jeremy Arblaster

EVIL RUNS IN THE FAMILY

HEREDITARY

~~KATHLEEN CHALFANT~~
|
TONI COLLETTE ──────────── GABRIEL BYRNE
|
ALEX WOLFF   MILLY SHAPIRO

A24   WRITTEN & DIRECTED BY
ARI ASTER

HEREDITARY

Alternative Poster by Jeremy Arblaster
Words by Toni Stanger

Ari Aster's distressing feature-length debut, *Hereditary*, came out of nowhere to absolutely blow everyone away. After Ellen, matriarch of the Graham family, passes away, her daughter's (Toni Collette) family begin to unravel, and terrifying secrets about their ancestry make their way to the surface. Aster has very quickly made a name for himself as the new lord of the horror-tragedy genre, especially with his equally harrowing sophomore feature, *Midsommar*.

Hereditary starts out like a ghost story, but evolves into something else entirely. Aster's genius comes from drawing inspiration from older generational films such as *Rosemary's Baby*, *Carrie* and *Don't Look Now*. The director masterfully blends horror tropes and supernatural elements with family drama, showing how the two go hand-in-hand. It is, in his own words, "a family tragedy that turns into a nightmare."

Although the film deals with a mixture of genres, the scariest parts of the film are those that are most familiar. Family dysfunction, brutal arguments, and grief add more grounded emotion to the true terror of real life.

Everything about the film plays with genre expectations, notably the camerawork, cinematography and performances (especially Collette, who was snubbed during Award Season). There is not a single thing working against *Hereditary*—it's the perfect horror film and it's a special one for us to have. To see a horror film as riveting and terrifying as this in our lifetime is a real treat.

dir. Ari Aster
with Toni Collette

Alternative Poster by Jeremy Arblaster

Alternative Poster by Maxime Pourchon

written for the screen and directed by Charlie Kaufman

Jesse Plemons   Jessie Buckley

i'm thinking *of* ending things

I'm Thinking Of Ending Things (2020)

dir. Charlie Kaufman
with Jessie Buckley, Jesse Plemons

Alternative Poster by Aisha Servia
Alternative Title Cards by Jeremy Arblaster

Alternative Posters by Sean Lazonby

Jessie Buckley • Toni Collette • David Thewlis • Jesse Plemons

written for the screen and directed by Charlie Kaufman

i'm thinking of ending things

a CHRISTOPH

INTERS

Interstellar Alternative Poster by Edward J Moran II

NOLAN film
TELLAR

Interstellar (2014)

Alternative Title Cards
Top: Angelina | Bottom: Jeremy Arblaster
Words by Yazz James

Growing up, I always loved sci-fi films, and was intrigued by space travel. Even now, I think that I might still take the risk of going up there—if I were ever offered. Perhaps that's why, despite not usually being Nolan's biggest fan, I can confidently say that *Interstellar* is one of my favourite films of all time.

For protagonist Cooper (Matthew McConaughey) his trip into space isn't a novelty; he's setting out to find a new planet to call home. A widowed father and former NASA pilot, he now lives on a decaying cornfield with his two children Murph (Mackenzie Foy, later Jessica Chastain) and Tom (Timothée Chalamet, later Casey Affleck).

At the heart of the film is the father-daughter bond between Murph and Coop, one that's stretched right across the infinite expanse of space and time. "Stay" she pleads, before he leaves the Earth's orbit, but, of course, he doesn't. Their goodbye ends with few words exchanged and the pair crying: the father from his truck and the daughter from the porch. It does not get less painful from there.

Adding to this is Zimmer's score. Always a careful balance between dramatic and heartfelt, Zimmer's compositions work well to evoke rising feelings of tension and anguish. Repeated motifs throughout the film bring the audience back down to Earth and portray a constant battle: what is best for mankind, and what is best for the individual? Hoyte van Hoytema's camerawork only accentuates this conflict more. Looming landscapes fill every inch of the screen, contrasted with invasive close-ups as the astronauts drift further away from their loved ones, mourning a life they can no longer live. Van Hoytema's shallow shots feel too private to be seen, placing the audience in close proximity to the characters as Nolan grounds an astronomical tale with human emotions.

Despite its run-time of almost three hours, Interstellar captivates, immersing the viewer for its entirety. It may be packed with sensation and spectacle, but this film still has soul. It is a story of selflessness and sacrifice.

dir. Christopher Nolan
with Matthew McConaughey, Jessica Chastain

a film by christopher nolan

STELLAR

INTERSTELLAR
a film from Christopher Nolan

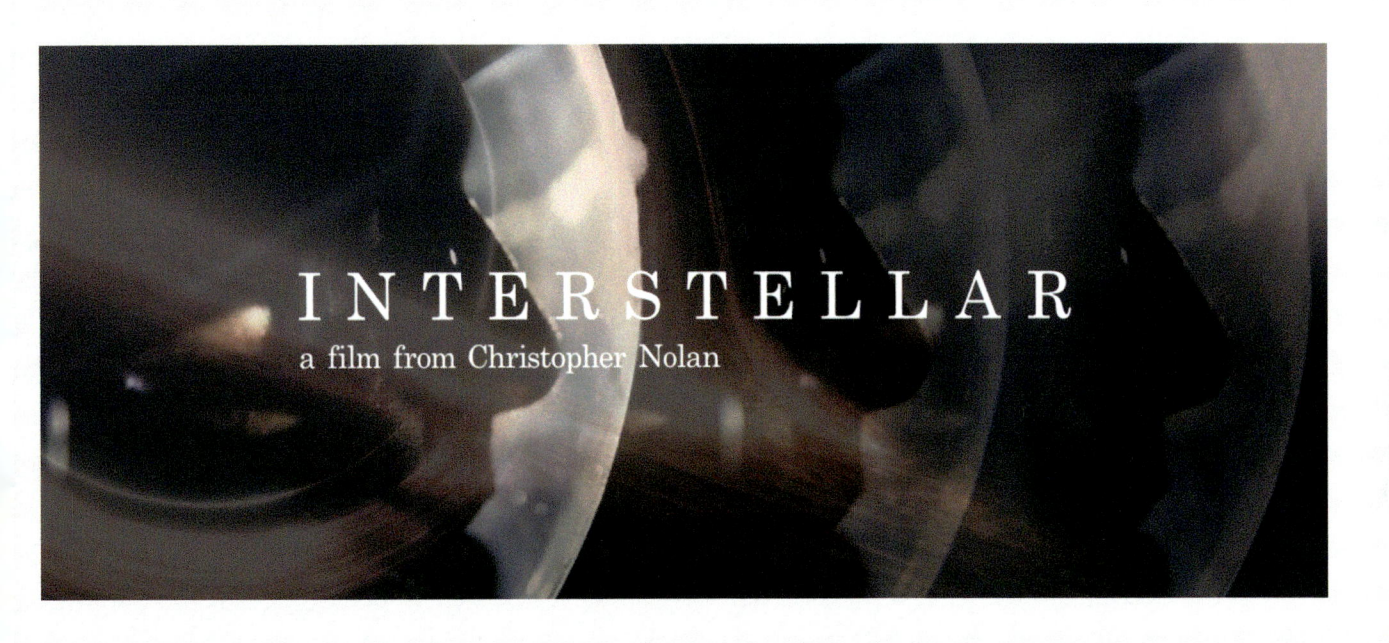

"Nolan asks... what's best for mankind, and what's best for the individual?"

The Irishman (2019)

Alternative Poster by Scott Saslow
Words by Harry Jones

It seems as though the world is fast becoming tired of the old guard. It's weary of so-called "bro" cinema, arguing it only tickles the fancies of young men looking to get off on the consequences of toxic masculinity: violence, crime, and misogyny. These very themes have been the subject of many a Martin Scorsese film. Despite this new skepticism towards an old formula, the director of *Mean Streets, Goodfellas, Casino* and *The Departed* wasn't shy to return to the world of gangsters in his contemplative epic, *The Irishman*.

That same dissenting voice was quick to dismiss *The Irishman* as a master treading familiar ground: an indulgent, star-studded, three-and-a-half-hour luxuriation that delivered more violence for the same old audiences. However, Scorsese has never been one to stagnate, and *The Irishman* is a colossal rumination on the frailty of lives surrounded by death. We follow mob hitman Frank Sheeran (Robert De Niro) as he finally reaches a conclusion he's already written for plenty of others.

It's a poignant, pensive meditation on ageing, forgiveness, and exiting this world with a bare-bones legacy. It turns out that it's exactly the kind of cinema we need.

dir. Martin Scorsese
with Robert De Niro, Al Pacino, Joe Pesci

"The Irishman is a colossal rumination of the frailty of lives surrounded by death."

"I heard you paint houses..."

ROBERT DE NIRO AL PACINO JOE PESCI

THE IRISHMAN

A MARTIN SCORSESE PICTURE

NATALIE PORTMAN

Jackie

A FILM BY
PABLO LARRAÍN

Jackie (2016)

dir. Pablo Larraín
with Natalie Portman

Alternative Poster by Alejandro Hinojosa
Alternative Title Cards by Jeremy Arblaster

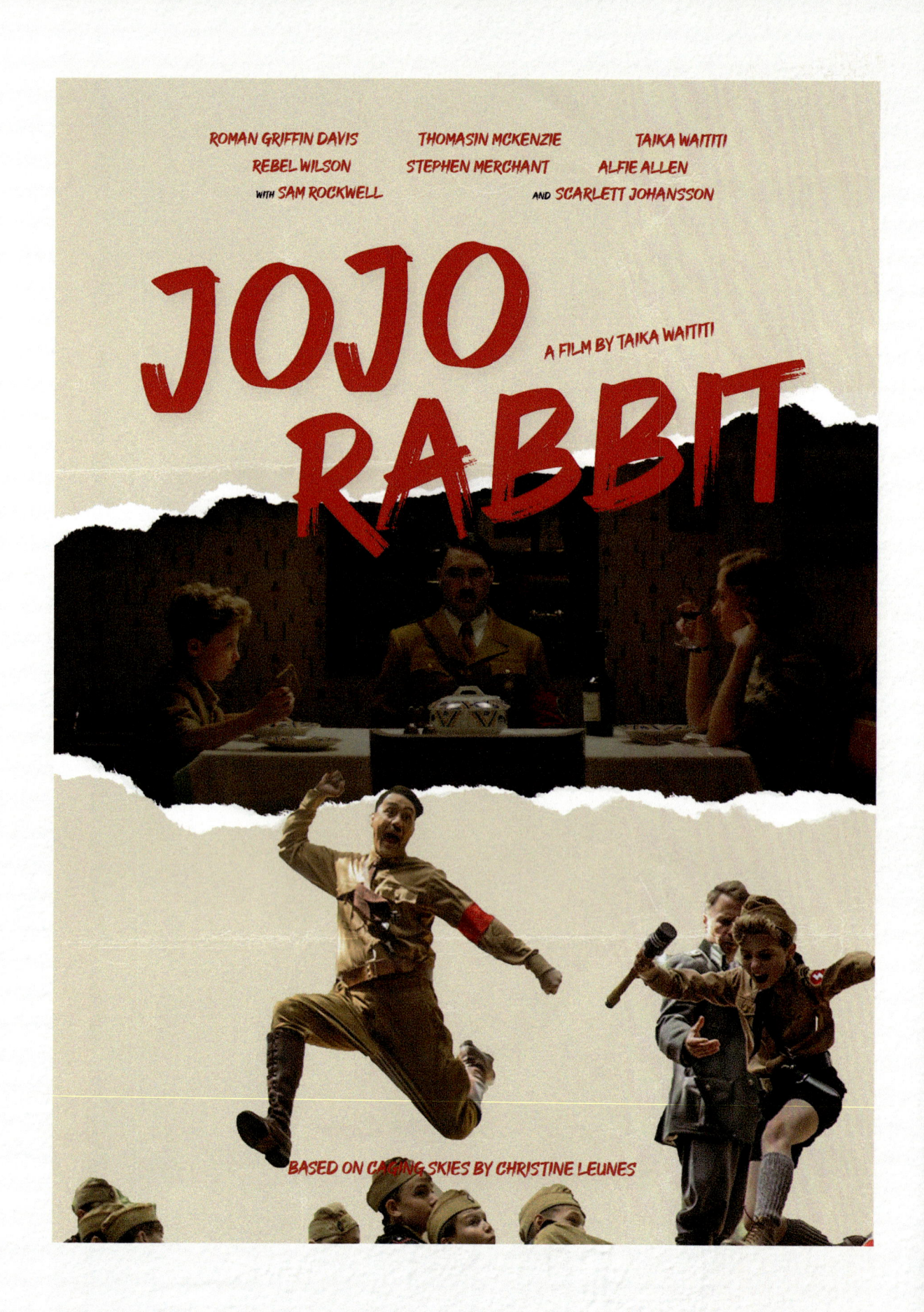

ROMAN GRIFFIN DAVIS　　THOMASIN MCKENZIE　　TAIKA WAITITI
REBEL WILSON　　STEPHEN MERCHANT　　ALFIE ALLEN
WITH SAM ROCKWELL　　AND SCARLETT JOHANSSON

JOJO RABBIT

A FILM BY TAIKA WAITITI

BASED ON CAGING SKIES BY CHRISTINE LEUNES

Alternative Posters by Gabriella Wintergrace & Ivan Zuniga

JOJO RABBIT

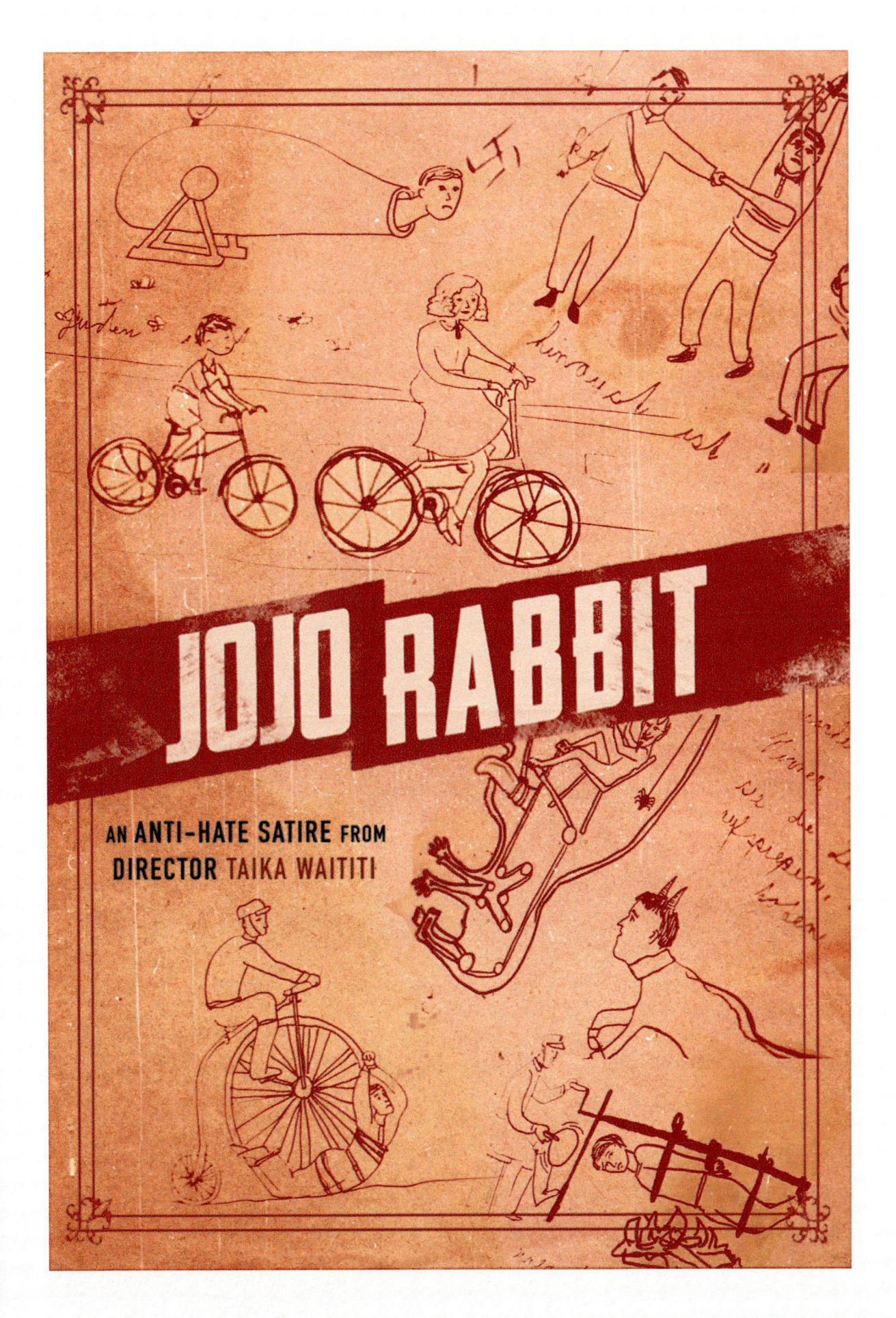

AN ANTI-HATE SATIRE FROM DIRECTOR TAIKA WAITITI

Knives Out (2019)

Alternative Poster by Dalal
Words by Josh Senior

The game is afoot as storied crime novelist Harlan Thrombey is found dead in the private study of his large family home, his jugular cut open as if he'd leapt from the pages of one of his own stories. His children, grandchildren and other dependents descend upon the estate, not only to grieve, but to keep a keen eye on his will and how his fortune will be divided.

The sprawling Thrombey family is jam-packed with despicable characters, each with enough motive to have done away with the family's patriarch. In classic whodunnit style, the characters are marched in — flaws and all—to speak with Cajun-detective Benoit Blanc (a career best from Daniel Craig) whose job it is to unravel the knots and discover the identity of the killer, helped by Harlan's devoted and intuitive nurse Marta (Ana de Armas).

And, whilst the film feels like a classic Hollywood crime caper, director Rian Johnson uses a variety of tricks, including a startling mid-act revelation, to create a film that feels fresh, daring and bold. The film twists and turns at breakneck speed, drip-feeding clues and hints, but never letting on its true direction.

With on-point performances and razor-sharp dialogue, the laughs are never too far away in a film that doesn't take itself too seriously. A great original script and star-studded cast that keeps its secrets well-hidden until the end, *Knives Out* is a rare cinematic treat. Rian Johnson invites you to play the game, and if you allow yourself to slip into suspended reality, you'll be justly rewarded.

dir. Rian Johnson
With Daniel Craig, Ana deArmas

"Rian Johnson uses a variety of tricks to create a film that feels fresh, daring and bold."

Everybody has a motive.
No one has a clue.

Knives Out

A Rian Johnson
Whodunnit

Daniel Craig - Chris Evans - Ana DeArmas - Jamie Lee Curtis - Michael Shannon - Don Johnson - Toni Colette - Lakeith Stanfield - Katherine Langford - Jaeden Martell - and Christopher Plummer

R RESTRICTED
UNDER 17 REQUIRES ACCOMPANYING PARENT OR ADULT GUARDIAN

THE LIGHTHOUSE

Alternative poster by Ahmad Sindi
Words by Emily Cashen

Story takes a backseat to mood in Robert Eggers' hypnotic second feature, *The Lighthouse*. A droning foghorn opens the film and sets the tone for what's to come—a relentless, intrusive, distressing sound that unsettles and torments.

It's this cacophony that greets our two wickies—Winslow (Robert Pattinson) and Wake (Willem Dafoe)—as they arrive at the remote, weather-beaten lighthouse that is to become their home for the next four weeks. Just as the sonic landscape disorientates and alarms, the film's distinctive visuals create a creeping sense of claustrophobia from the opening frame. Shot in a boxy 1.19:1 aspect ratio, the film traps our wickies in a tight, square image, creating an uneasy feeling that the walls are closing in around them.

Rain lashes the desolate island, a one-eyed seagull makes a menacing appearance, and sea shanties are drunkenly sung by candlelight. As the two men find themselves marooned by worsening weather, paranoia, distrust and delusions erupt into episodes of violence and hallucination. This briny, booze-soaked marvel has safely solidified Eggers as one of the most exciting filmmakers of the future.

dir. Robert Eggers
with Willem Dafoe, Robert Pattinson

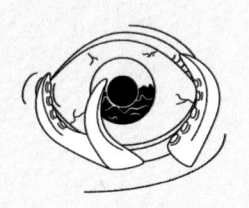

"As the sonic landscape disorientates and alarms, the film's distinctive visuals create a sense of claustrophobia."

Illustration by Isabelle France

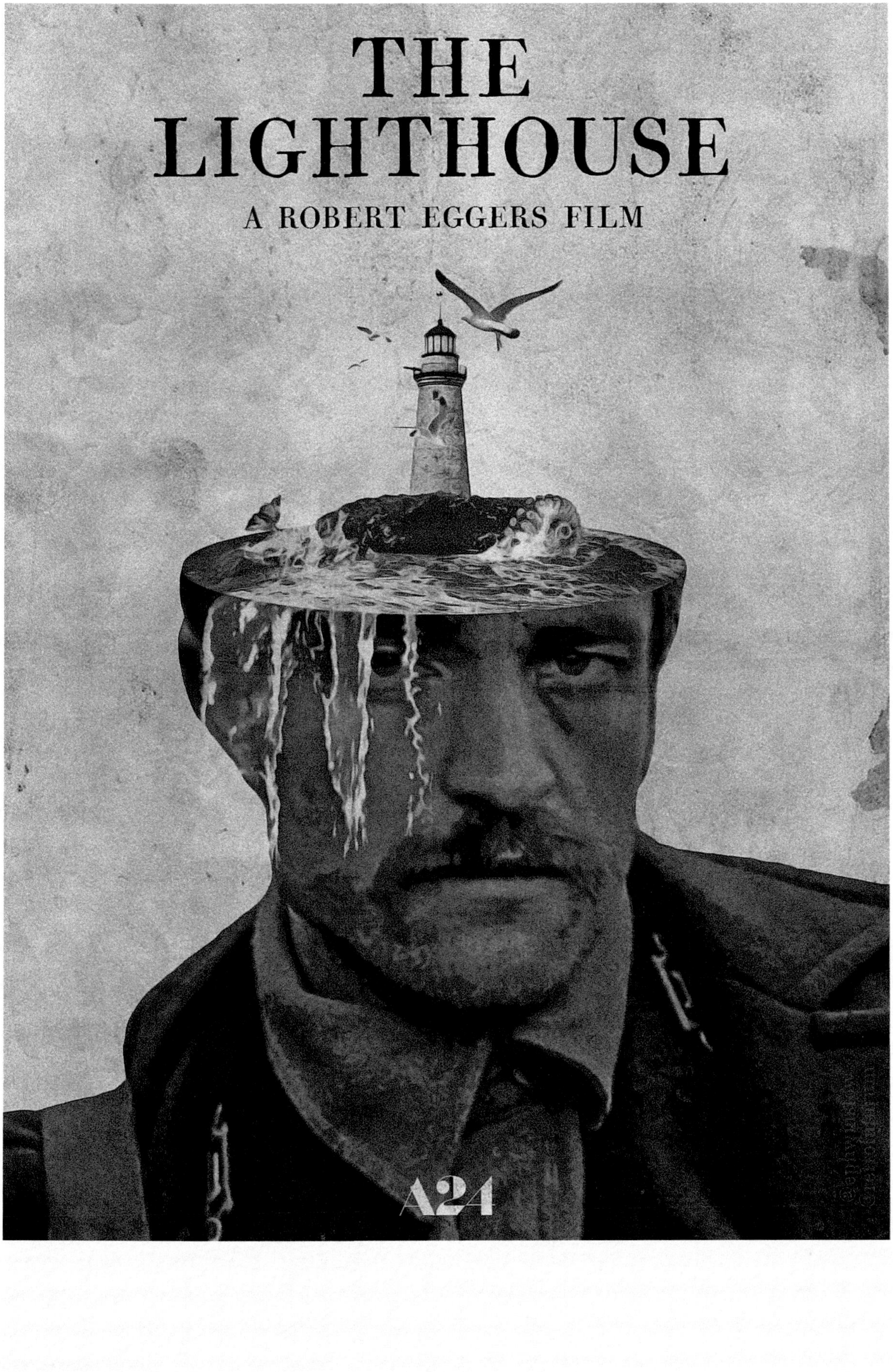
THE
LIGHTHOUSE
A ROBERT EGGERS FILM
A24

KEEPING
SECRETS
ARE YE?

WILLEM DAFOE   ROBERT PATTINSON

THE
LIGHTHOUSE

DIRECTED BY
ROBERT EGGERS

THE LIGHTHOUSE

WILLEM DAFOE & ROBERT PATTINSON

A24

Alternative Posters by Scott Saslow & Jeremy Arblaster

Alternative Character Posters by Gabriella Wintergrace

Willem DAFOE

THE
LIGHT
HOUSE

a film by Robert Eggers

A24

Little Women (2019)

Alternative poster by Scott Saslow
Words by Charlotte J

Little Women is a luminous evocation of memory and identity. All elements move harmoniously in sync between Louisa May Alcott's original text and the modernity of Greta Gerwig's direction. This is at once a delicate cinematic object and a sweeping adaptation of the well-known coming of age material, serving as a true eye-opener about the strengths, passions, and socio-economic standpoints of women. It is a story that genuinely moves its audience, with true clarity and heart—Gerwig understands the story so well you could almost mistake it for her own work.

Each actor bounces effortlessly off one another, deriving raw emotion and feelings from their characters, as they explore their nuances with warmth and charm. Likewise, the cinematography is vibrant with rich colours soaking every frame.

Little Women is a timeless story, still influential for young women even so many years after the book's release, and this refresh is a fantastic use of the classic novel, reshaping the humour, rough times and heart-wrenching twists for a modern audience.

It teaches us that life has its setbacks, but that it will always surprise us with what good can come from those. *Little Women* grips you with the warm embrace of a good hug.

dir. Greta Gerwig
with Saoirse Ronan, Emma Watson, Florence Pugh, Timothée Chalamet,

"A story that moves its audience with true clarity and heart."

SAOIRSE RONAN
EMMA WATSON
FLORENCE PUGH
ELIZA SCANLEN
LAURA DERN
TIMOTHÉE CHALAMET
AND MERYL STREEP

Little Women

Alternative Poster by Sean Lazonby

Little Women

Louisa May Alcott

Alternative Book Cover by Beth Morris

比爾・默里

LOST IN TRANSLATION

Film by Sofia Coppola

斯嘉麗・約翰遜

Lost In Translation (2003)

Alternative Poster by Daniel Deme
Words by Emily Cashen

Lost in Translation is a film perfectly suspended between sleeping and waking life. A deceptively simple story of two lonely souls forming a connection in a place far from home, Sofia Coppola's 2003 sophomore project takes its time in bringing our two leads together. We meet Bob (Bill Murray) and Charlotte (Scarlett Johansson) separately, finding them both isolated, disorientated and utterly adrift in their respective lives – feelings compounded by the unfamiliar city that engulfs them and the sleeplessness they suffer.

While Bob and Charlotte's prior interactions with the city and the people that surround them are defined by miscommunication and disconnection, their conversations with one another are easy, intimate and unflinchingly honest. As they spend more time in each other's company, days, hours and minutes begin to fade into each other, with the couple entering something of a dreamworld, a shared reality born from their unlikely emotional connection.

Days and nights pass in a haze of half whispered conversations that can only happen with a perfect stranger at 3am halfway around the world. These moments of intimacy are rendered all the more magical for their fleeting, ephemeral nature. Both Bob and Charlotte know that before too long, the spell will be broken, and they will have to leave their dreamworld to return to reality, but for now, they both feel seen and understood, in a way that transcends the transient.

dir. Sofia Coppola
with Bill Murray, Scarlett Johansson, Tokyo

"A deceptively simple story of two lonely souls forming a connection."

Alternative Posters by Jeremy Arblaster

4
ANSCO SAFETY FILM
GARY OLDMAN
IS
Mank
FROM DAVID FINCHER
CAFE
BRONSON AVE.
700 N.
NETFLIX

The Master (2012)

Alternative Poster by Sam Coyle
Words by Brianna Zigler

In Paul Thomas Anderson's post-WWII masterpiece—about charismatic cult leaders, male sexuality, and the struggles faced by veterans reintegrating into society—sight, sound, and career-defining performances collide to make *The Master* arguably Anderson's artistic zenith.

The film follows loner Freddie Quell (Joaquin Phoenix) as he faces difficulties in returning to a home that no longer exists for him, following his service in the Navy.

Traumatised, sexually voracious and addicted to alcohol, after stumbling through failed jobs he finds himself accidentally in the welcoming arms of a magnetic man named Lancaster Dodd (Phillip Seymour Hoffman)—leader of a burgeoning philosophical movement that call themselves "The Cause."

Taken by Freddie's strange, wayward behaviour and his potent concoction of homemade moonshine, Dodd takes Freddie in as a new member of The Cause and attempts to mould him into one of his disciples.

But Freddie's penchant for deviance, erraticism, and violent outbursts puts him at odds with Dodd's wife, Peggy (Amy Adams), and The Cause's other members, as he develops a zealous devotion to Dodd in his desperate desire for a place where he belongs.

Previously described by Anderson as his favourite film he's made, it's a mystifying amalgamation that has yet to be fully cracked, though undoubtedly a beautiful and uncomfortable examination of masters, masculinity, and the fruitless search for meaning in the meaningless.

dir. Paul Thomas Anderson
with Joaquin Phoenix,
Phillip Seymour-Hoffman

THE MASTER *a* PAUL THOMAS ANDERSON *film*

Alternative Poster & Title Card by Jeremy Arblaster
Alternative Title Cards (Top & Bottom) by Yudhistira Reihan

THE MASTER
written and directed by PAUL THOMAS ANDERSON

The Master
From Paul Thomas Anderson

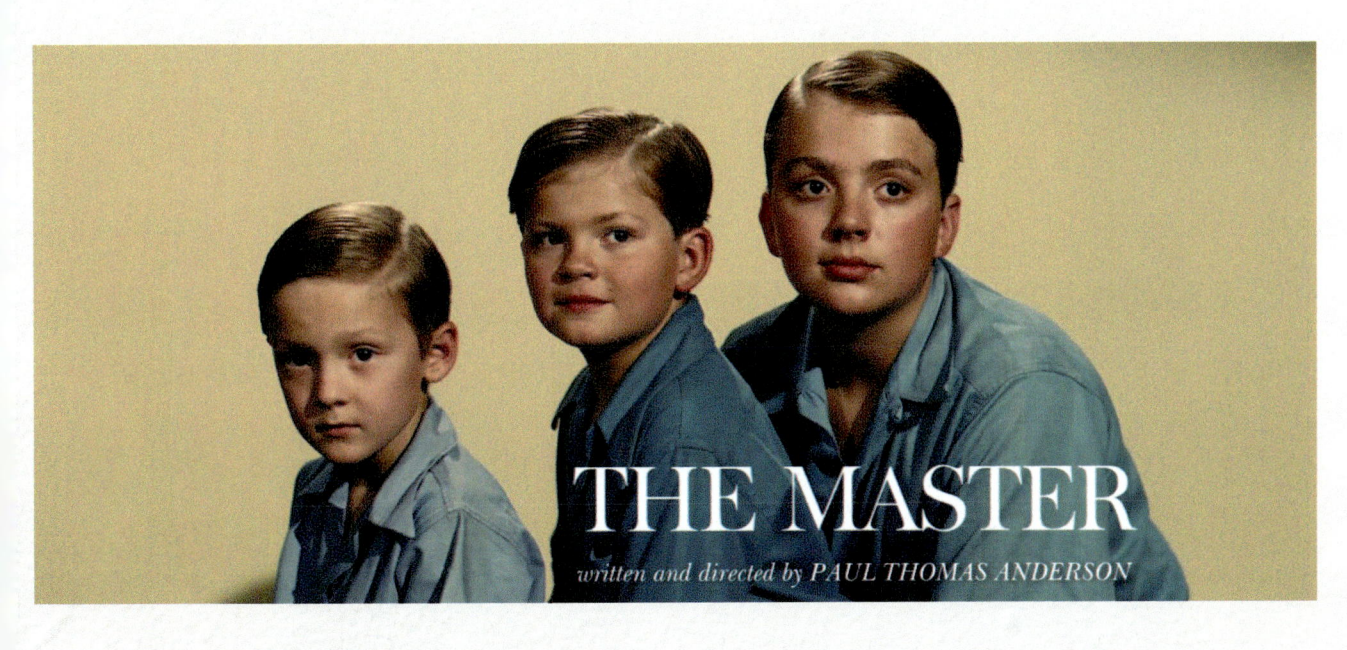

THE MASTER
written and directed by PAUL THOMAS ANDERSON

Alternative Poster by Gabriel Murgueytio

Midsommar (2019)

dir. Ari Aster
with Florence Pugh

Alternative Title Card by Gabriella Wintergrace
Words by Jeremy Arblaster

With a striking visual identity, *Midsommar* has proved to be an immensely popular film for experienced and budding designers alike to channel their creative talent. Gabriel Murgueytio's flyer-poster for *Midsommar* is a wonderfully playful way to introduce us to Ari Aster's imagined Scandinavian cult where, amongst never-ending daylight and starched white clothes, their obsession with purity is rooted in classic antiquated European ideals and a perversion of Nordic culture.

Wallace McBride's stunning alternative poster for *Midsommar* perfectly captures the way Dani's sense of reality begins to disintegrate, as she falls deeper into the sinister Swedish cult. But surrounded by her new-found family and with her grief and trauma dissipating , Dani blossoms.

Alternative posters by Wallace McBride & Luke Headland

from ARI ASTER
director of HEREDITARY
MIDSOMMAR
A24
ART BY LUKE HEADLAND
R

MOONLIGHT

Alternative Poster by Ahmad Sindi
Words by Blaise Radley

Easily the finest Best Picture winner in a generation, *Moonlight* is a staggering achievement; a quiet bulldozer of blue-suffused heartache. The tale of a young Black man struggling with alternate modes of absent paternity, school-yard bullies, and the expectations that lead him to forcibly define his own identity, it's the rare coming-of-age piece that recognises growing up is far from a linear path.

It's no surprise Jenkins followed *Moonlight* with an adaptation of a James Baldwin novel, since so many of the same issues of the self that plagued Baldwin's writing are present here. More than that though, Jenkins frames his work in the manner of a novelist, laying out three key chapters in the life of Chiron that chart lines of thought without offering definitive answers.

Jenkins' authorly impulses are quickly forgotten behind the camera, with each frame shot by cinematographer James Laxton effortlessly communicating the tumult lying beneath Chriron's calm seas. Defined as much by the mood of moonlit waters as by the little things he does say, Jenkins' dexterous hand solidifies Chiron as one of modern cinema's most subtly layered protagonists. *Moonlight* isn't just a poignant window into the lives of African-Americans in South Florida—it's a soothing balm for the soul.

dir. Barry Jenkins
with Trevante Rhodes, André Holland

"Moonlight isn't just poignant – it's a soothing balm for the soul."

MOONLIGHT
A FILM BY BARRY JENKINS

TREVANTE RHODES ASHTON SANDERS MAHERSHALA ALI NAOMIE HARRIS

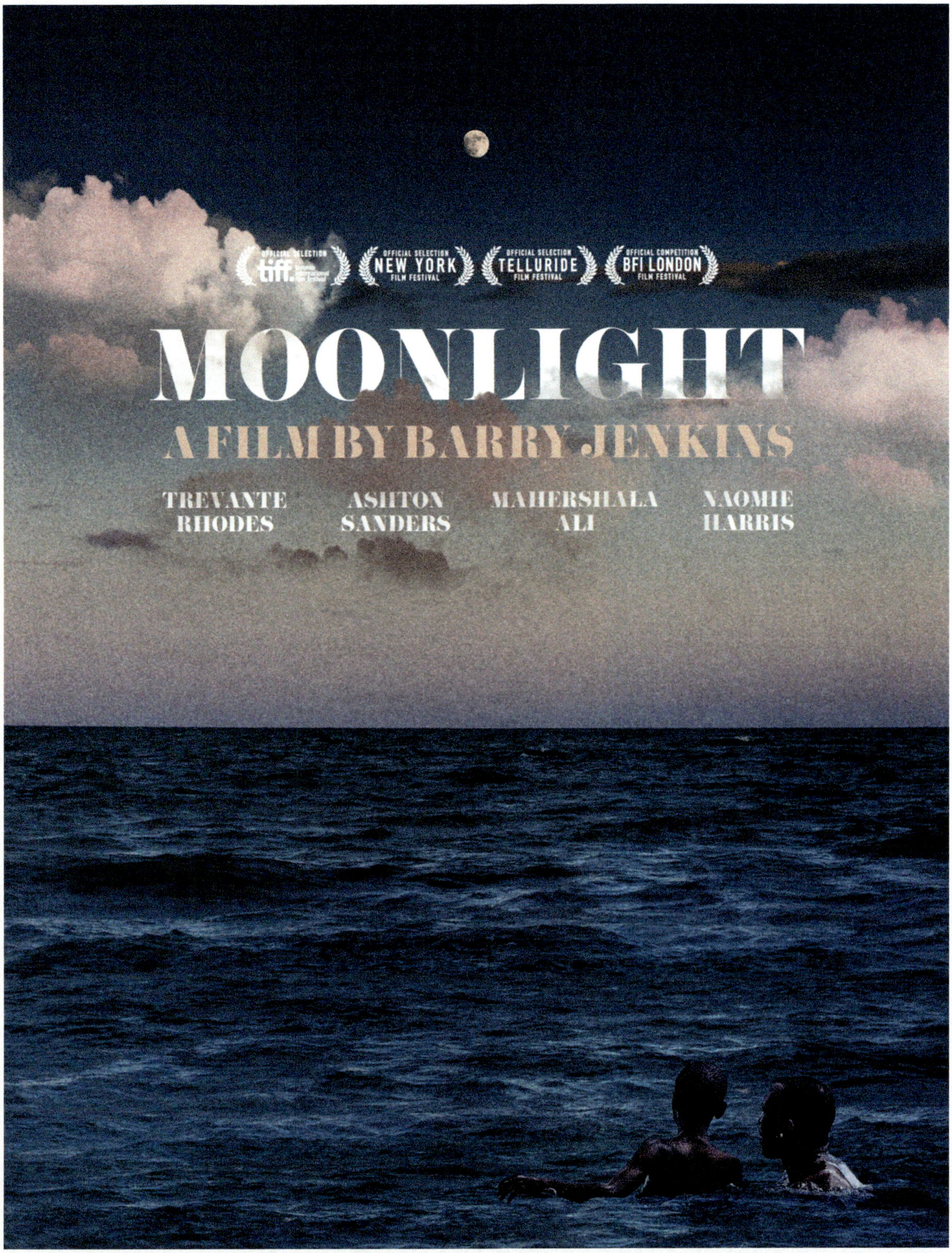

MOONLIGHT
A FILM BY BARRY JENKINS
THIS IS THE STORY OF A LIFETIME

Alternative Poster by Louie Baharom
Alternative Title Cards:
Top: Clémence Agenet
Bottom: Gabriella Wintergrace

THERE ARE NO CLEAN GETAWAYS
NO COUNTRY FOR OLD MEN
A COEN BROTHERS MOVIE

No Country For Old Men (2007)

Alternative Poster by Mathieu David
Words by Harry Jones

The Coen brothers' Best Picture winner is somewhat of an anomaly in their filmography. Though no strangers to violence, broad characterisation and people falling into trouble they never bargained for, the Coens usually lend a large dose of black comedy to their pulpier movies. If there is any dark humour to be taken away from *No Country For Old Men*, then it's so pitch black that it's near impossible to distinguish from the rest.

Adapted from Cormac McCarthy's seminal novel of the same name, the Coens manage to blend their well-established brand of exciting, dilemma-ridden films with McCarthy's brooding tale of greed and fear, finding something true to both their own work and the source material.

Like many Coen and McCarthy characters, Javier Bardem's Anton Chigurh is a man at odds with society, seemingly acting purely on the nature that drives him. Bardem's performance, which won him the Oscar for Best Supporting Actor, is a searing, straight-faced nightmare, and one of the most iconic performances of the century.

dir. Joel & Ethan Coen
with Javier Bardem, Josh Brolin, Tommy Lee Jones, Kelly Macdonald

"The Coens blend their brand of dilemma-ridden film with McCarthy's brooding tale of greed and fear."

Nocturnal Animals (2016)

Alternative Poster by Rafal Rola
Words by Matthew Floyd

Life is art for filmmaker and luxury fashion designer Tom Ford. Casting his hyper-stylised eye behind a camera lens for only the second time, *Nocturnal Animals* is texturally and thematically bold, both a challenging exercise and delicious satire. Amy Adams is Susan Morrow, the architect of her own gilded cage as the wealthy owner of an LA art gallery, consciously closing off her own creativity in pursuit of traditional Western markers of success: loaded pockets, fancy friends, and a dashing husband.

What pulls the rug from beneath her in vivid fashion is a manuscript from her estranged ex-husband Edward Sheffield.

Channelling their fallout into a spectacularly unsettling fiction that reflects their shared history, Jake Gyllenhaal dually plays resentful writer Sheffield and imagined, ineffectual Tony Hastings—both a far cry from his action-heartthrob persona.

Ford's premise brilliantly uses a film within a film to explore the limits of the artform, playing with the audience's suspension of disbelief with the confidence of a man whose career does not depend on it. Have faith in Ford that no brushstroke is unintended.

dir. Tom Ford
with Amy Adams, Jake Gyllenhaal

> "Casting his hyper-stylised eye behind the camera, Nocturnal Animals is texturally and thematically bold."

NOCTURNAL ANIMALS

A FILM BY
TOM FORD

Once Upon a Time in...Hollywood (2019)

Alternative Poster by Rafael Orrico Diez
Words by Matthew Floyd

Nobody walks in Hollywood. It's February 1969, the movie business is changing, the hippie revolution is afoot, and the Manson cult is on the rise. Tarantino shows us all of this, but not through Sharon Tate, Steve McQueen or any real-world instrumental figure. Instead, we follow the fictional Rick Dalton, a fading western star, and his loyal stuntman Cliff Booth, as they bum around town, sniffing out the next job and a stiff drink.

Something of a late-career opus, this is Tarantino firmly in his wheelhouse, building such a textured portrayal of '69 Hollywood that you can smell the car-seat leather—and there's plenty of opportunity to do so. Like his characters, we spend a lot of time behind the wheel.

Big studio pictures were the run of the day, which meant a lot of hanging around. You're either at work or driving to work. If you're not working, you're driving to meetings and parties that could land your next part.
Once Upon A Time in...Hollywood is a hang-about movie with a subversive grounding in infamous history, the joy here is in the journey.

dir. Quentin Tarantino
with Leonardo DiCaprio, Brad Pitt, Margot Robbie, Feet

"A late-career opus, a textured portrayal of Hollywood in 1969. You can smell the car-seat leather."

ONCE UPON A TIME IN... HOLLYWOOD

Leonardo DiCaprio.............................as *Rick Dalton*
Brad Pitt...as *Cliff Booth*
Margot Robbie...................................as *Sharon Tate*
Emile Hirsch.......................................as *Jay Sebring*
Margaret Qualle............................... "ussycat"

Columbia Pictures presents in association with Bona Film Group Co., LTD. and a Heyday Films production.

By Quentin Tarantino starring Leonardo DiCaprio Brad Pitt Margot Robbie.

casting by Victoria Thomas, csa costume designer Arianne Phillips film editor Fred Raskin, ACE production designer Barbara Ling director of photo. Robert Richardson.

Executive producers Georgia Kacandes Yu Dong Jefrey Chan produced by David Heyman Shannon McIntosh written and directed by Quentin Tarantino.

Release date May 21, 2019 (Cannes)

Distributed by Sony Pictures Releasing

Quentin Tarantino

Running time 161 minutes

FESTIVAL DE CANNES

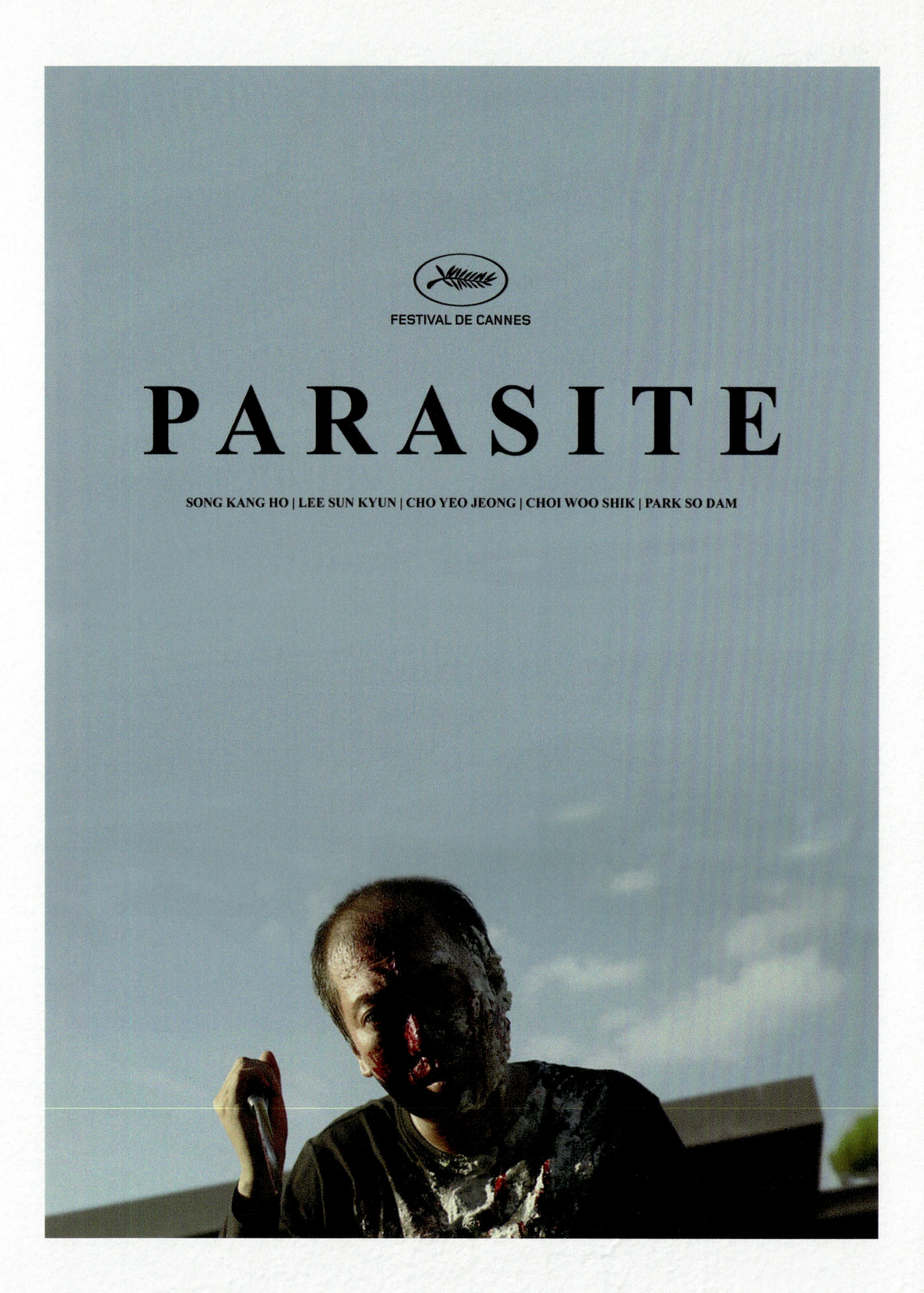

PARASITE

SONG KANG HO | LEE SUN KYUN | CHO YEO JEONG | CHOI WOO SHIK | PARK SO DAM

Alternative Posters by Reggie Azwar

P A R A S I T E

FESTIVAL DE CANNES

A FILM BY BONG JOON-HO

SONG KANG HO
LEE SUN KYUN
CHO YEO JEONG
CHOI WOO SHIK
~~PARK SO DAM~~

Alternative Posters by Jeremy Arblaster

FESTIVAL DE CANNES
BEST SCREENPLAY

Adèle Haenel   Noémie Merlant

PORTRAIT
OF A
LADY
ON FIRE

A film by
Céline Sciamma

A Quiet Place (2018)
Words by Megan Christopher

Sometimes you want a film to just destroy your nerves, and John Krasinski's *A Quiet Place* does just that and a whole lot more. Set in a post-apocalyptic world where the remaining humans are hunted by monsters, this sci-fi horror provokes fear purely in its concept: whilst being hunted by extraterrestrial life forms is bad enough, these aliens have perfect hearing. In order to save their lives and the lives of their children, Lee (John Krasinski, who also directs) and Evelyn (Emily Blunt) must remain as quiet as possible at all times.

It would have been easy to simply rely on jump scares, but the true horror of *A Quiet Place* is found in the silence in-between. Krasinski, alongside writers Bryan Woods and Scott Beck, come up with ingenious ways of stretching this terrifying idea to its absolute limit, utilising childbirth, cochlear implants and the natural disobedience of young children to illustrate just how difficult lifelong silence would be. Through playing on an intrinsic fear, *A Quiet Place* is a great example of just how intelligent and creative horror can be.

Book Cover from Good Movies as Old Books by Matt Stevens

Good Movies as Old Books is exactly as it sounds. A beautiful collection of great films, reimagined as old book covers by the incredibly talented Matt Steves.
A sound investment!

dir. John Krasinski
with John Krasinski, Emily Blunt, Monsters

A Quiet Place

John Krasinski

ROMA

A FILM BY ALFONSO CUARÓN

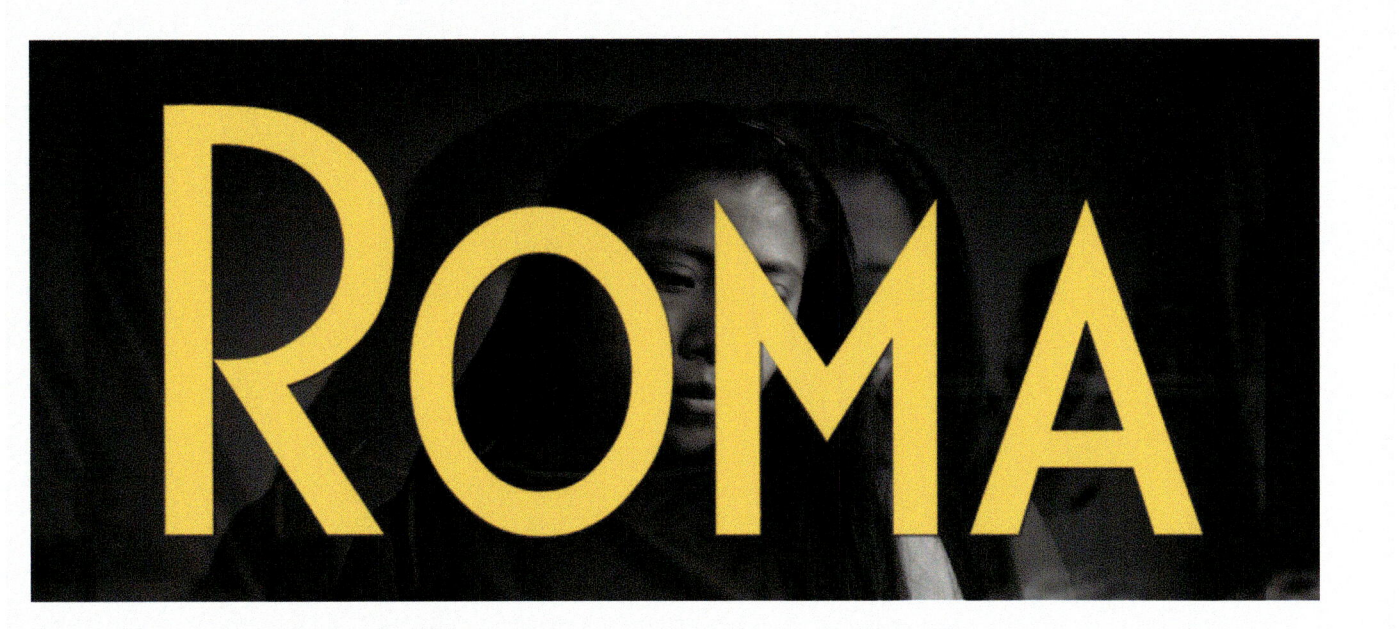

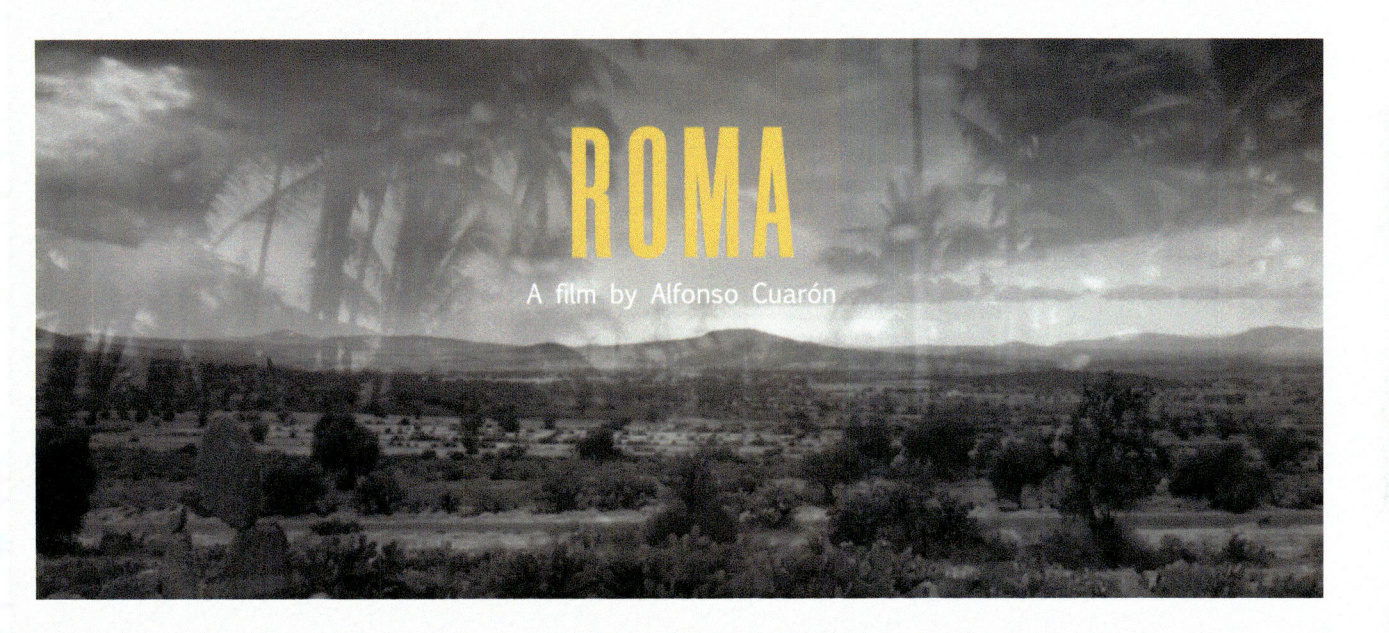

Roma (2018)

dir. Alfonso Cuarón
with Yalitza Aparicio

Alternative Poster by Heemin Chun
Alternative Title Cards by Jeremy Arblaster

SAINT MAUD

Alternative Poster by Cassandra Kuek
Words by Jeremy Arblaster

Romans 13:13-14
Make no provision for the flesh, to gratify its desires.

In *Saint Maud* the viciousness of the Bible is brought to life when a private nurse attempts to "save" the soul of her patient, an enigmatic former dancer whose body has been taken over by cancer — one of God's cruellest tricks. Amanda represents all that must be saved; a confident, sophisticated, sexually-fluid woman, with a bohemian lifestyle. As her new nurse, the devout Maud finds this lifestyle totally reprehensible and vows to set Amanda on the path to repentance.

Maud though, has her own secrets. A violent past is revealed almost immediately, as debut director Rose Glass shows us just enough to offset Maud's kindlier actions. And with this glimpse we see how Maud fits into a wider liberal narrative—that those most conservative in thought are simply denying their inner-most desires. Though their initial relationship seems built on mutual intrigue, the chasm between their beliefs comes quickly into view as their connection mutates, winding through sexual tension, frustration and jealousy, into fear, anger, and finally into aggression.

Proverbs 16:27
Idle hands are the devil's workshop; idle lips are his mouthpiece.

Maud's frenzied fanaticism puts her at odds with Amanda and the world around her. Isolated and unemployed in a small town, we see how easily Maud slips into radicalisation, a theme that plays on our fears of fundamentalism in any form.

Nothing exemplifies this more than Morfydd Clark's physical, balletic performance as Maud. Natural thoughts and desires become warped and contorted as she gives herself up to a higher power. Her utterances turn to whispers and speaking in tongues. The natural becomes supernatural. As we reach the dramatic, celestial finale, the last glimpse of Maud will burn brightly, however you feel.

dir. Rose Glass
with Jennifer Ehle, Morfydd Clark, God

Philippians 2:15
Then you will shine among them like stars in the sky...

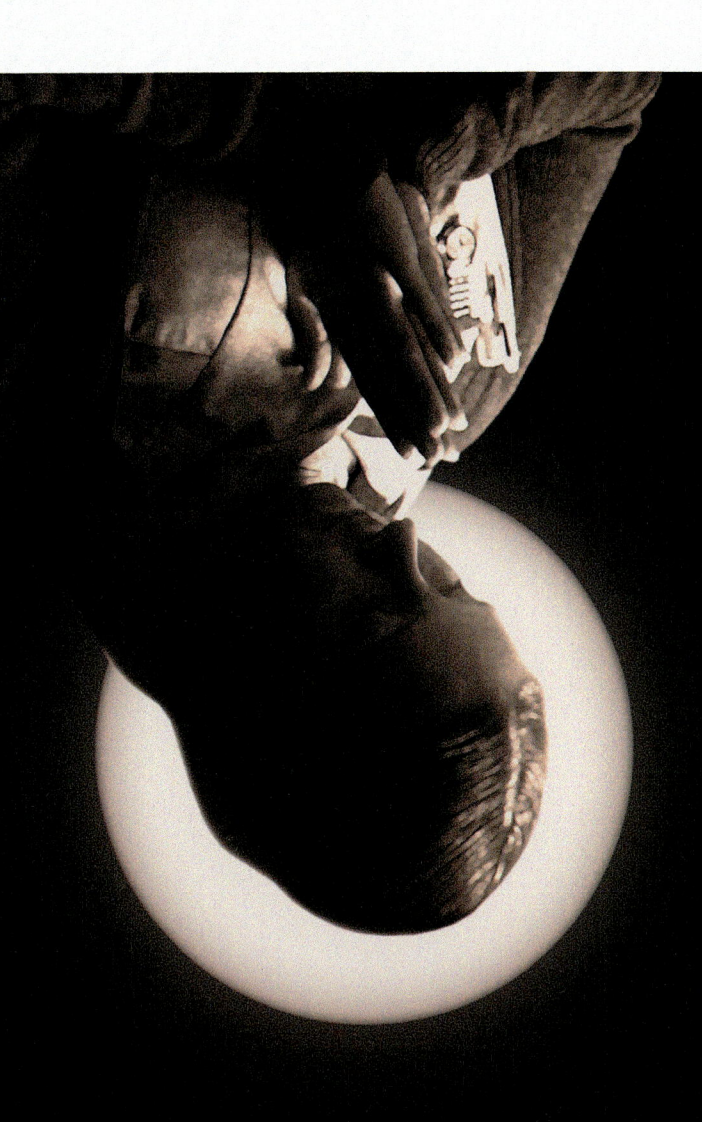

SAINT MAUD

a film by ROSE GLASS

Alternative Poster by Darren Tu

Alternative Poster by Sean Lazonby

SHAME

Alternative Poster by Jeremy Arblaster
Words by Blaise Radley

Oh bless the humble pervert, forever fated to be associated with criminals and predators, even if his predilections are taboo rather than unconscionable. That's not to say Brandon Sullivan (Michael Fassbender), the subject of Steve McQueen's character piece, *Shame*, isn't reprehensible, but rather that his sexual deviance is as much the subject of our empathy as it is morally questionable. You won't find many passionate embraces here.

Shame is a suitably awkward fit as a title, one that speaks to the remorse Brandon should feel, and he does—in fleeting moments. But Brandon's actions are far from penitent. Whether masturbating in his office toilets, or ogling exhibitionists going at it against their high rise window, Brandon finds pleasure at every opportunity his cold corporate life affords him. That is, until anyone in his personal life confronts him about his habits.

Like with *Hunger*, McQueen shows a preternatural ability to unpack the grotty edges of human existence, but where *Hunger* was driven by the rage of dogmatic martyrs, *Shame* holds its emotions at a distance; at first, anyway. As Brandon pursues his depraved desires ever-more desperately, the gap between us and him closes, and in the end we're left with a beating, sweaty heart, and the memory of Fassbender's flaccid member.

dir. Steve McQueen
with Michael Fassbender, Carey Mulligan

"Shame unpacks the grotty edges of human existence."

a Steve McQueen film

SHAME

michael fassbender
carey mulligan

There Will Be Blood

A Film by Paul Thomas Anderson

Daniel Day-Lewis

Paul Dano

There Will Be Blood (2008)

Alternative Poster by Heemin Chun
Words by Brianna Zigler

Based loosely on Oil!, the 1927 novel by Upton Sinclair, Daniel Day-Lewis stars in *There Will Be Blood* as the inimitable megalomaniac Daniel Plainview in his quest for power and oil in California at the turn of the 20th century.

After starting off as a silver prospector and eventually discovering oil, the accidental death of a worker at a drilling site allows Plainview to adopt the man's orphaned son and use him to promote a façade of "family values" in future business dealings. Thus, Plainview works his way up the economic food chain in an America brimming with potential prosperity for those willing to pull up their bootstraps. But Plainview's voracious desire for accumulating as much wealth and influence as possible hits a strange crossroads when he meets charismatic pastor Eli Sunday (Paul Dano), whose family Plainview cons into giving over their oil-rich land.

In its portrayal of greed, existentialism, exploitation—of both people and the environment—and false prophets, Paul Thomas Anderson's stark, unrelenting portrait of America's fraught relationship with capitalism perverts the "American Dream." Paired with Johnny Greenwood's score and Robert Elswit's sweeping cinematography, Day-Lewis's chilling embodiment of undaunted avarice is both towering and pitiful, as Plainview favours material gain over human empathy to his own bleak end.

dir. Paul Thomas Anderson
with Daniel Day Lewis, Paul Dano

"An unrelenting portrait of America's fraught relationship with capitalism."

UNCUT GEMS

Directed by
Ben Safdie and
Joshua Safdie

PREMIERE   2019   A24   UNCUT GEMS   DECEMBER 25

Adam Sandler	'Everything I
Julia Fox	do, it's not
Kevin Garnett	going right, and I don't know what to do.'
Idina Menzel	Sahar Bibiyan
Keith Stanfield	Sean Ringgold
Eric Bogosian	Paloma Elsesser
	Pom Klementieff
Judd Hirsch	John Amos
The Weeknd	Keith Williams Richards

A24 PRESENTS

A24 A PICTURE "UNCUT GEMS" STARRING ADAM SANDLER JULIA FOX LAKEITH STANFIELD KEVIN GARNETT IDINA MENZEL ERIC BOGOSIAN JUDD HIRSCH AND ABEL TESFAYE ORIGINAL SCORE BY DANIEL LOPATIN EXECUTIVE PRODUCERS MARTIN SCORSESE EMMA TILLINGER KOSKOFF OSCAR BOYSON ANTHONY KATAGAS AND DAVID KOPLAN

PRODUCED BY SCOTT RUDIN, P.G.A. ELI BUSH, P.G.A. AND SEBASTIAN BEAR-MCCLARD, P.G.A. WRITTEN BY JOSH SAFDIE BENNIE SAFDIE AND RONALD BRONSTEIN DIRECTED BY JOSH SAFDIE AND BENNY SAFDIE   DECEMBER 25,   2019

Uncut Gems

Alternative Poster by Rafael Orrico Diez
Words by Blaise Radley

Under neoliberalism, you are an asset. As an asset, you work to acquire further, supplementary assets, improving your own worth (not by much) until suddenly Life is Good; if you're a real salt-of-the-earth, bootstrap-pulling worker ant, that is. For the Safdie Brothers, our profit motive is a festering sickness, one that contorts and distorts ambitions into ones and zeros, but it's also a sick joke—the kind you have to laugh at for its farcical totality.

Accordingly, the principal focus of *Uncut Gems*, Howard Ratner (Adam Sandler), is simultaneously a neoliberal's wet dream and their most deformed nightmare. A skeevy, morally unscrupulous jewellery peddler, Howie swears and sweats almost as much as he wheels and deals. No offer is ever good enough, no win ever big enough, to sate his materialist hungers—if he had the Midas touch, even his loved ones would end up gilded.

The paradox posed by the Safdies is born of Sandler's inherent charm. Howie's a sleazeball, sure, objectionable, absolutely, and yet as he brushes past each climax to the next gamble, you can't help but grip your fingernails in, praying he'll pull the parachute cord. Either an anxious-wreck of a thriller or a cacophonous comedy depending on your disposition, *Uncut Gems* finds the absurdity in imagining humanity has any numeric worth.

dir. Josh & Benny Safdie
with Adam Sandler, Julia Fox,
KG aka 'The Big Ticket'

"No offer is ever good enough, no win ever big enough..."

UNDER THE SKIN

Alternative Poster by Jeremy Arblaster
Words by Laura Venning

Jonathan Glazer's *Under the Skin* is a sharp slice of metaphysical surreality that, like *2001: A Space Odyssey* (which it echoes in its opening), transports us to the edge of human existence. But it also peels back layers and burrows deep, exploring what it means to live in a woman's skin.

Scarlett Johansson's alien woman who trawls the streets of Glasgow is beautiful, as women are supposed to be, and sensuous, as women are supposed to be. But she's also a predator with a coat of brown fur that prowls in a white van, who men aren't afraid of because they haven't learned to be afraid of smiling strangers quick to ask personal questions and pat the seat next to them.

Her hunger and her cruelty as her prey are swallowed by a pitch-black liquid abyss is shocking. But there is both triumph and tragedy in watching her consume those men who would have consumed her.

We all sometimes feel alien, and the film is both a viscerally unsettling sci-fi horror and a deeply empathetic portrait of loneliness. What's humanity if not the connections we form with other humans?

dir. Jonathan Glazer
with Scarlett Johansson

"A viscerally unsettling sci-fi horror and a deeply empathetic portrait of loneliness."

Scarlett Johansson

UNDER

THE

SKIN

a film by
Jonathan Glazer

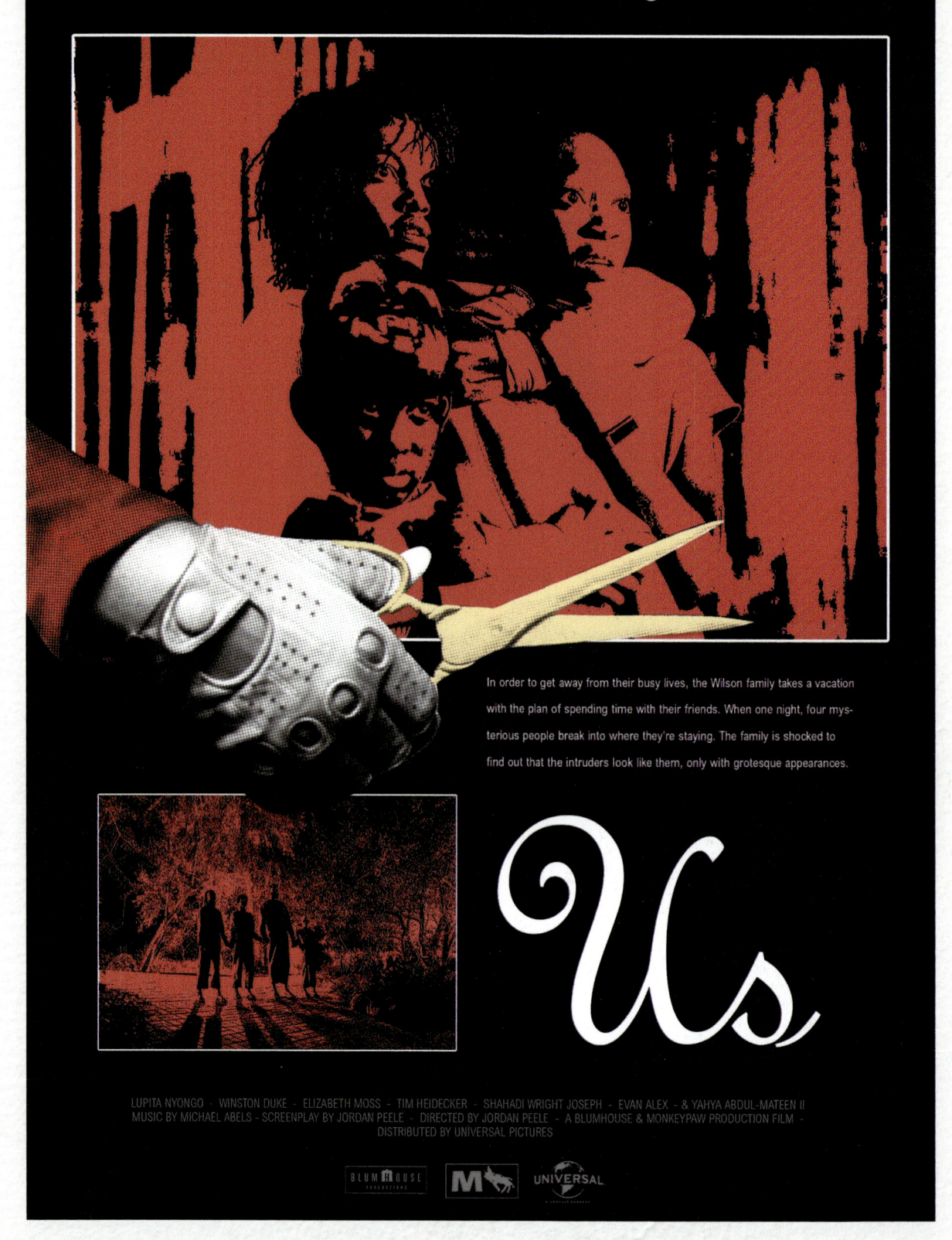

Alternative Poster by Dalal

Alternative Poster by Adam Juresko

Natalie Portman

VOX LUX

Alternative Poster by Henrique Ferreira Fernandes

Alternative Poster via FanArt.TV

THE VVITCH

Alternative Poster by Adam Juresko
Words by Blaise Radley

Somewhere around the middle-half of the 20th century, unknown regions ceased existing. Space: seen; Earth: explored; folklore: dismissed. For the average person in 2021, life's most pressing questions have all but been wrapped up in a neat bow. And yet, instinctive fears remain. Even as our always-on digital lives see us explain away abnormalities, the power of horror filmmaking lies in tapping into something primal; the uncanny underbelly. Needless to say, there are no neat bows in Robert Eggers terrifying debut *The Witch*.

Released in an era where horror films increasingly lean on metaphorical terrors and ambiguity, *The Witch* is unashamedly throwback. At its heart is a literal witch, or even a coven of them, the sort that lurk on the periphery of human endeavour, manipulating events and torturing the bewildered and misguided. It's a confirmation of every ghoulish tale adult minds attempt to put to rest.

Set in 17th century New England, Eggers mines his period piece for all its worth, his cast of sullen-faced puritans talking exclusively in archaic colloquialisms. As much about the horrors of frontier life as infanticidal blood magic practitioners, *The Witch* manages to be thematically rich while also turning stomachs. Regardless of its glacial pacing, this is a legitimately chilling feature that adroitly taps into the quiet fears modern society has painted as foolish.

dir. Robert Eggers
with Ralph Ineson, Anya Taylor-Joy

the VVitch
A New England Folktale

Ex_Machina (2015)

Alternative Poster by Tom Sheffield
Words by Blaise Radley

Welcome to a parallel dimension. No, not the near-future corporate utopia hinted at in *Ex_Machina*, but the Phonetic A-Z Alternative Poster Book where *X_Machina* was the project of director/writer Alex Garland. This is what it feels like to step through the looking glass.

If that sort of shallow thought exercise isn't your cup of tea, then Garland's brand of "what if?" storytelling will probably leave you high and dry. But for those looking for a knotty but grounded cerebral thriller, *Ex_Machina* effectively and consistently twists the knife.

Centring on just three characters, this is science fiction stripped back to its most barebones, harkening back to lower budget macabre mysteries a la Twilight Zone, or that Charlie Brooker show. Our audience surrogate is Caleb Smith (Domnhall Gleeson), coding grunt for Google-parallel Blue Book, who wins a lottery to visit the home of his alcoholic-cum-spiritualist billionaire boss, Nathan Bateman (Oscar Isaac). Only, not is all as it seems.

Nature encroaches on every foot of Nathan's home; mountain sides bursting into his lounge, and foliage growing up the exterior walls — a clear contrast with the clinical design of his underground laboratories. Burning low and slow, this tale of creators and creations; humanity and nature; "intelligent" men and artificial intelligence, swirls with contrasts and ambiguity. If that wasn't enough, it also features one of the finest dance sequences of the decade—proof smart films shouldn't be afraid to be a little dumb.

dir. Alex Garland
with Domnhall Gleeson, Alicia Vikander
Oscar Isaac

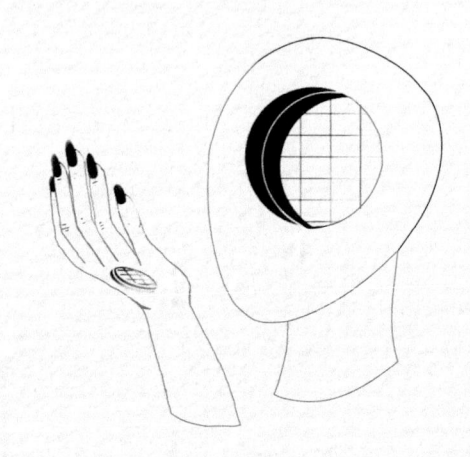

Illustration by Isabelle France

AN ALEX GARLAND FILM

EX MACHINA

THERE IS NOTHING MORE HUMAN THAN THE WILL TO SURVIVE

YOU WERE NEVER REALLY HERE

You Were Never Really Here weighs heavy on the mind, its sag reflected in the bloated barrel-chest of hired gun Joe (Joaquin Phoenix). Forever grimacing or rippling, Joe cuts a brutal shape, but you sense that's a far cry from how he wants to define himself. Every decisive act of violence he takes feels marred by guilt, even as he holds himself at a distance. Each bloody bludgeoning, and each splattered headshot is pushed off-frame or viewed through a further mediary, tying us to the dissociated state of a lifelong victim of abuse.

We live as much in Joe's memories as in his present, transitioning between the two as if slipping through the cracks in his psyche. Paired with Lynne Ramsay's fondness for partially-focused close-ups, it's a disorienting watch, even as each washy memory is rooted in real time triggers. Joe's recollections aren't flights of fancy—they're provocations from his environment, or premonitions of the consequences his actions might beget. Never has a man with such an aggressive penchant for hammers felt so worthy of empathy.

dir. Lynne Ramsay
with Joaquin Phoenix

"Every act of violence feels marred by guilt."

Alternative Poster
by Jay Bennett
Words by Blaise Radley

JOAQUIN PHOENIX
YOU WERE NEVER REALLY HERE
A FILM BY
LYNNE RAMSAY
WHY NOT PRODUCTIONS PRESENTS A FILM4 & BFI FILM "YOU WERE NEVER REALLY HERE" STARRING JOAQUIN PHOENIX EKATERINA SMASONOV JUDITH ANNA ROBERTS ALESSANDRO NIVOLA ALEX MANETTE JOHN DOMAN CASTING BY BILLY HOPKINS & ASHLEY INGRAM COSTUME DESIGN BY MALGOSIA TURZANSKA PRODUCTION DESIGN BY TIM GRIMES MUSIC BY JOHNNY GREENWOOD EDITED BY JOE BINI CINEMATOGRAPHY BY THOMAS TOWNEND CO-PRODUCER CARRIE FIX EXECUTIVE PRODUCER JONATHAN AMES JACQUES AUDIARD LIZZIE FRANCKE ROSE GARNETT BEN ROBERTS SUE BRUCE SMITH PROCUDED BY ROSA ATTAB PASCAL CAUCHETEUX REBECCA O'BRIEN LYNNE RAMSAY JAMES WILSON BASED ON THE BOOK BY JONATHAN AMES WRITTEN BY LYNNE RAMSAY
WHY NOT PRODUCTIONS

Alternative Poster by Rafael Orrico Diez

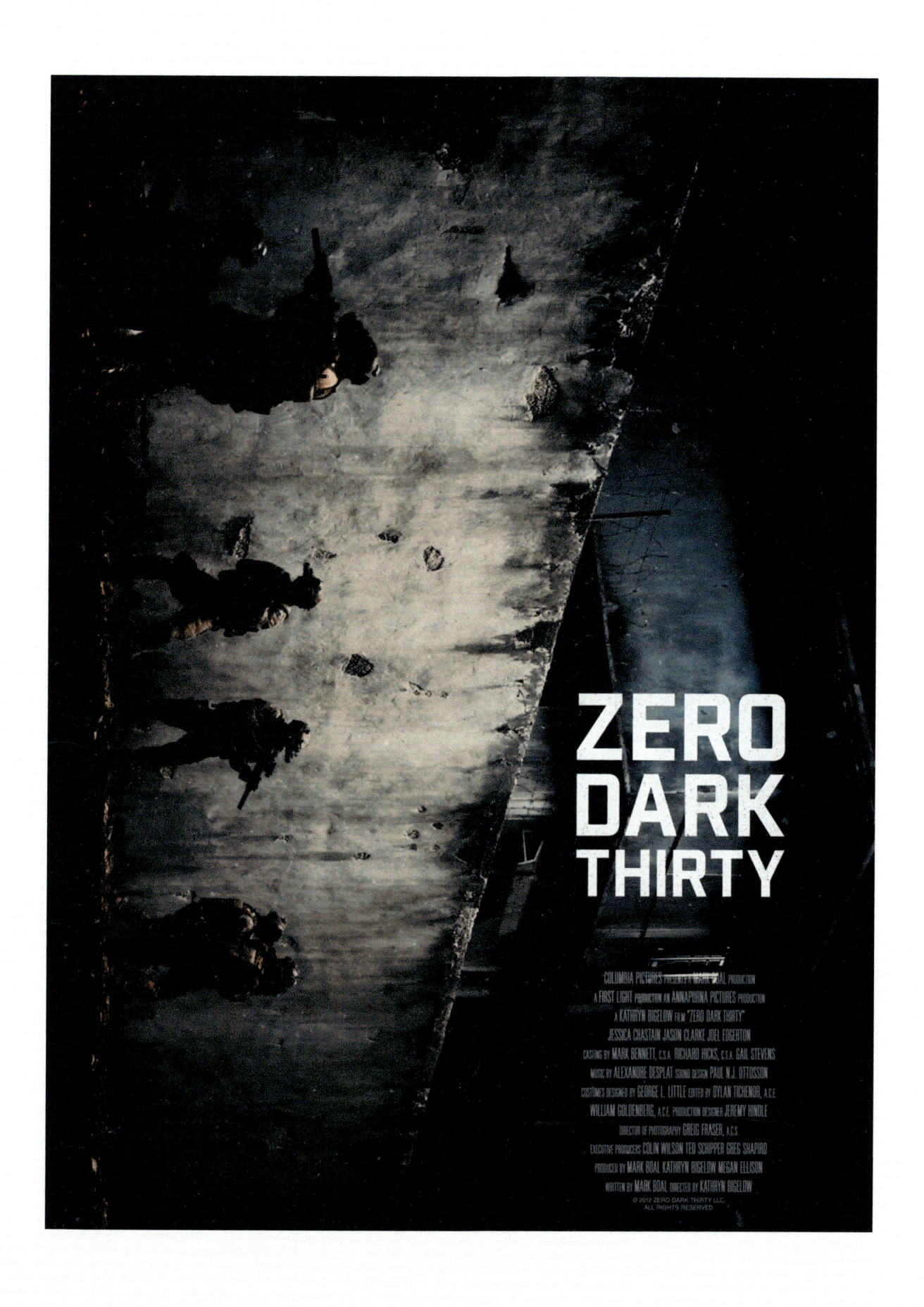

Alternative Poster by Scott Saslow

DESIGN

Designer	Twitter	Instagram
Clémence Agenet	@voxxlux	@cl.em.ence
Angelina	@w0ngkarwais	@angelinason_
Jeremy Arblaster	@jeremyarblaster	@jeremyarblaster
Arden Avett	@ardenavett	@ardenavett
Reggie Azwar	@ysrdal	@regsstudio
Louie Baharom	@loubaharom_	@ayeeitslou
Jay Bennett	@yajpeg	@yajpeg
Heemin Chun	-	@hmimimin
Sam Coyle	@samcoyledesign	-
Dalal	-	@designsverse
Mathieu David	-	@mathieudavid_
Henrique Ferreira Fernandes	-	@h_____ff
Alex Finney	@xelafinney	@xelafinney
Lara Flesch	-	@laraflesch
Isabelle France	@isabelleafrance	@iaf_illustration
Cassie Friel	-	@cassiusviolet
Julia Harto	@filmtasha	-
Luke Headland	@photoshophorroz	@horrorposterarts
Alejandro Hinojosa	@alecxps	@alecxpsdesign
Jiho	@hyeongskarwai	-
Adam Juresko	@nosupervision	@nosupervision
Cassandra Kuek	-	@fragiledesignco
Sean Lazonby	@seaniobeanio	@sean_lazonby
Santana López	@herrozzy	@herrozzy

SOCIALS

Wallace McBride	@cousinbarnabas	@unlovelyfrankenstein
Agustin R. Michel	@agustinrmichel	@agustinrmichel
Maryse Mikhail	-	@ninetyfourgraphik
Edward J Moran II	-	@edwardjmoran
Beth Morris	@_bamcreate	@_bamcreate
Gabriel Murgueytio	-	@gabicus
Matt Needle	@needledesign	@needledesign
Rafael Orrico Diez	@diezorrico	@rafaorricodiez
Alexis Payán	@luhxxs	-
Maxime Pourchon	-	@maximepourchon
Yudhistira Reihan	@yudhismr	-
Rafa Rola	@rolarafal	@rolarafal
Scott Saslow	@saslow_scott	@scottsaslow
Aisha Servia	@sanktaisha	@aishtark
Tom Sheffield	@cybersheff	@cybersheff_art
Ksenia Shliakhtina	-	@ksenia.shliakhtina
Ahmad Sindi	@writtenbyahmad	@retrofuturum
Ken Sjöberg	@sjobergfilm	@kensjoberg
Matt Stevens	@mattstevensclt	@mattstevensclt
Mariana Tineo B.	-	@emtibi_
Darren Tu	-	@void_endeavours
Anton Volk	@antovolk	@antovolk
Gabriella Wintergrace	@avocadobarnes	@wintergrce
Bren Zonneveld	-	@movueposters
Ivan Zuniga	@iz_designs	@iz_designs

WEB

Clémence Agenet	linktr.ee/clemonpluto
Angelina	letterboxd.com/filmgirlthot
Jeremy Arblaster	behance.net/jeremyarblaster
Arden Avett	posterworks.co.uk
Reggie Azwar	madebyreg.tumblr.com
Louie Baharom	cinephiliaph.wordpress.com
Jay Bennett	jaybennett.me
Sara Clements	muckrack.com/sara-clements
Sam Coyle	samcoyledesign.com
Mathieu David	mathieudavid.fr
Alex Finney	behance.net/alex-finney
Lara Flesch	laraflesch.com
Trudie Graham	trudiegraham.contently.com
Julia Harto	letterboxd.com/birdsofvenus
Luke Headland	lukeh01.redbubble.com
Alejandro Hinojosa	behance.net/alecxpsdesign
Yazz James	yazzjames.contently.com
Adam Juresko	adamjuresko.com
Santana López	cargocollective.com/herrozzy
Wallace McBride	unlovelyfrankenstein.com
Maryse Mikhail	behance.net/marysemikhail
Edward J Moran II	society6.com/edwardjmoranii

WEB

Beth Morris	bamcreate.co.uk
Gabriel Murgueytio	gabrielmurgueytio.com
Matt Needle	mattneedle.co.uk
Rafael Orrico Diez	rafaorrico.com
Maxime Pourchon	maximepourchon.fr
Blaise Radley	blaiseradley.journoportfolio.com
Peyton Robinson	peytonrobinson.com
Rafa Rola	rafalrola.pl
Scott Saslow	scottsaslow.myportfolio.com
Aisha Servia	aisharchives.carrd.co
Tom Sheffield	jumpcutonline.co.uk
Ksenia Shliakhtina	behance.net/kseniashliakhtina
Ahmad Sindi	retrofuturum.com
Ken Sjöberg	behance.net/sjobergstudio
Toni Stanger	linktr.ee/tonistanger
Matt Stevens	hellomattstevens.com
Mariana Tineo B.	mtineob.cargo.site
Darren Tu	behance.net/darrentu
Laura Venning	lauravenning.contently.com
Gabriella Wintergrace	behance.net/gwintergrace
Brianna Zigler	briannazigler.contently.com
Ivan Zuniga	cargocollective.com/rzdesigns

WRITING

Contributor	Twitter
Jeremy Arblaster	@jeremyarblaster
Emily Cashen	@emilycshn
Sara Clements	@mildredsfierce
Meg Christopher	@tinyfilmlesbian
Matthew Floyd	@mattjfloyd
Isabelle France	@isabelleafrance
Trudie Graham	@_trudiegraham
Nick Griffin	@gick_niffin
Charlotte J	@charlojett
Yazz James	@oncleyazz
Harry Jones	@harryijones
Blaise Radley	@radleyblaise
Peyton Robinson	@peytondani
Josh Senior	@joshsenior90
Toni Stanger	@wescravn
Laura Venning	@laura_venning
Brianna Zigler	@justbrizigs

Alternative Film Posters A-Z

Follow us
@az_filmposters

ARTCIRCUS
BOOKS

BV - #0018 - 270121 - C149 - 280/200/10 [12] - CB - 9781913425814 - Matt Lamination